Lying

LYING

A
METAPHORICAL
MEMOIR

LAUREN SLATER

RANDOM HOUSE NEW YORK

RANDOM HOUSE and colophon are registered trademarks
of Random House, Inc.

Grateful acknowledgment is made to Alfred A. Knopf, a division of
Random House, Inc., for permission to reprint seventeen lines of poetry
from *The Gold Cell* by Sharon Olds. Copyright © 1987 by Sharon Olds.
Reprinted by permission of Alfred A. Knopf, a division of Random
House, Inc.

ISBN 0-375-50112-6

Random House website address: www.atrandom.com
Printed in the United States of America on acid-free paper
9   8   7   6   5   4   3   2

First Edition

Book design by Barbara M. Bachman

For Tyler and Weld—
in gratitude

I first encountered Lauren Slater as a writer when I read her account of schizophrenia in her book *Welcome to My Country*. Since that time I have followed her work, always intrigued by its development. Now, in her third effort, this author brings us a daring meditation on creative nonfiction, a story of epilepsy that is at once entertaining and disturbing. What makes this book disturbing is its incrementally rising refusal to state the facts of the illness about which she writes. By the end of the book, the reader is, indeed, left to wonder whether, or to what degree, Ms. Slater has suffered epilepsy, or if she has used the disease as a meaningful metaphor to convey what are otherwise unutterable experiences in her life.

Using metaphor as a literary technique is not a new concept in fiction; however, using, or suggesting, the use of metaphor as a valid vehicle to convey autobiographical truths—thus her insistence that this book is, indeed, a nonfiction memoir—is a new and unsettling idea. Perhaps more unsettling and exciting is the writer's insistence on not revealing to us which aspects of her disease are factual, which symbolic, which real, which fantastical, and by doing so asking us to enter with her a new kind of Heideggerian truth, the truth of the liminal, the not-knowing, the truth of confusion, which, if we can only learn to tolerate, yields us greater wisdom in the long run than packaged and parceled facts.

This book requires courage, along with an open and flexible mind. I have been disturbed, widened and exhilarated by my reading of it, as I hope you will be too.

Hayward Krieger
Professor of Philosophy
University of Southern California

The classic grand mal attack, such as this youth suffers, may be divided into four distinct stages. One, the onset. Two, the rigid state. Three, the convulsive stage. Four, the stage of recovery. During stages two and three, the main treatment must be to prevent the convulsion from injuring the patient. There is no fear at this stage of him injuring other people, though the relaxing of the sphincter and the contracture of the abdominal musculature may cause incontinence. A wooden gag should be placed between the teeth before they become clenched, to prevent the patient from either biting himself or those who are assisting him. During stage two, and before stage three has been reached, the clothing should be loosened and the head, the arms, and the legs laid firmly on the ground, with pressure continued for the duration.

FROM *The Text Book of Grand and Petite Mal Seizures in Childhood,* 1854

PART ONE

ONSET

I exaggerate.

CHAPTER 2

THREE BLIND MICE

The summer I turned ten I smelled jasmine everywhere I went. At first I thought the smell was part of the normal world, because we were having a hot spell that July, and every night it rained and the flowers were in full bloom. So I didn't pay much attention, except, after a while, I noticed I smelled jasmine in the bath, and my dreams were full of it, and when, one day, I cut my palm on a piece of glass, my blood itself was scented, and I started to feel scared and also good.

That was one world, and I called it the jasmine world. I didn't know, then, that epilepsy often begins with strange smells, some of which are pleasant, some of which are not. I was lucky to have a good smell. Other people's epilepsy begins with bad smells, such as tuna fish rotting in the sun, dead shark, gin and piss; these are just some of the stories I've heard.

My world, though, was the jasmine world, and I told no one about it. As the summer went on, the jasmine world grew; other odors entered, sometimes a smell of burning, as though the whole house were coming down.

Which, in a way, it was. There were my mother and my father, both of whom I loved—that much is true—but my father was too small, my mother too big, and occasionally, when the jasmine came on, I would also feel a light-headedness that made my mother seem even bigger, my father even smaller, so he was the size of a freckle, she higher than a house, all her hair flying.

My father was a Hebrew School teacher, and once a year he took the *bimah* on Yom Kippur. My mother was many things, a round-robin tennis player with an excellent serve, a hostess, a housewife, a schemer, an ideologue, she wanted to free the Russian Jews, educate the Falashas, fly on the Concorde, drink at the Ritz. She did drink, but not at the Ritz. She drank in the den or in her bedroom, always with an olive in her glass.

I wanted to make my mother happy, that should come as no surprise. She had desires, for a harp, for seasonal seats at the opera, neither of which my father could afford. She was a woman of grand gestures and high standards and she rarely spoke the truth. She told me she was a Holocaust survivor, a hot-air balloonist, a personal friend of Golda Meir. From my mother I learned that truth is bendable, that what you wish is every bit as real as what you are.

I have epilepsy. Or I feel I have epilepsy. Or I wish I had epilepsy, so I could find a way of explaining the dirty, spastic glittering place I had in my mother's heart. Epilepsy is a fascinating disease because some epileptics are liars, exaggerators, makers of myths and high-flying stories. Doctors don't know why this is, something to do, maybe, with the way a scar on the brain dents memory or mutates reality. My epilepsy started with the smell of jasmine, and that smell moved into my mouth. And when I opened my mouth after that, all my words seemed colored, and I don't know where this is my mother or where this is my illness, or whether, like her, I am just confusing fact with fiction, and there is no epilepsy, just a clenched metaphor, a way of telling you what I have to tell you: my tale.

...

The summer of the smells was also the summer of new sounds. There were the crickets, which I could hear with astonishing clarity each evening, and the rain on the roof, each drop distinct. There was the piano, which my mother did not tell us about, her secret scheme, delivered one day in ropes and pulleys, its forehead branded "Lady Anita."

"Return it," my father said.

"I can't," she said. "I've had it engraved."

"Anita," he said. We were standing in the living room. "Anita, there's no room to move with this Steinway in here."

"Since when do you move anyway?" my mother said. "You play pinochle. You pray. You are not a man who requires room."

I never witnessed one of their fights. My father was, by nature, private and shy. My mother, though flamboyant, did

not display emotion in public. Whenever a fight came up I
was banished to my room. I, however, had long ago discovered that if I put my head in the upstairs bathroom toilet
bowl, I could hear everything through the pipes.

"We can't afford this," I heard my father say.

"You," my mother said, "had the chance to partner up in
Irving Busney's bakery business."

And so it went from there, as it always did, fights con-
taining words like *you,* and *you,* fights about bills and house
repairs, vacations and cars, fights with false laughs—ha! and
ha! and sometimes crashing glass, and other times, like this
time, such silence.

. . .

And in the silence—a silence of moments, hours, days—my
mother started to play. A strange thing happened then. I
could see the sounds she made, the high piano notes pink and
pointed, the low notes brown and round. I don't mean this
metaphorically. I watched the colors and I watched my
mother. She had no talent, but she didn't stop. A driven
woman, my mother never knew the way time might slow in
a tub, the pleasure of a stretch. I watched her hands arched,
her neck stiff, and I felt my eyes go fuzzy and saw spectrums
in the room, colors much more beautiful than the sounds
from which they sprang, her repetitive rhythms, twinkle
twinkle little star, and three blind mice, bonking and chasing
their tails.

And then one day, as the mice were being blind, I went
with them. My sight shut down; it was black; I could not see.

"Mom," I said. I held on tight to the side of the piano.

"I'm practicing," I heard her say.

"Mom," I said. "I can't see."

She stopped. "Of course you can see," she said. "You have two eyes. You can see."

"It's dark," I shouted.

"How many fingers am I holding up?" she asked.

"I can't see your fingers," I said.

"Of course you can see my fingers," she said. "You have two eyes. Now look."

I felt her grip my chin, force my face toward her. "How many fingers? *Think.*"

I heard some panic in her voice now, but not a lot, because my mother believed you could conquer anything through will.

"Two," I said, a total guess.

"Exactly," she said, triumphant.

And just like that, I started to see again. She said *exactly* and the angles came back, as though her words determined the truth and not the other way around, the way it should be: something solid.

. . .

I could see again, most of the time fine, but not always. First I smelled jasmine, and then I had whole moments when the world went watery, when I saw the air break apart and atomize into dozens of glittering particles. Ahead of me shapes and colors suggested the billowing sails of a ship, or a zebra floating, when in reality it was just a schoolgirl in the crosswalk. I had not known, until then, that beauty lived beneath the supposedly solid surface of things, how every line was really a curve uncreased, how every hill was smoke.

At first the vision problems frightened me because I thought I was going blind, but as weeks went by, I settled in. I thought of the vision the same way I thought of the smells, as a secret world. I became dreamy, sometimes hours and hours passing, and afterward, although I hadn't been asleep, I would feel I was waking, and my head hurt.

This is how epilepsy begins. It begins beautifully, and with only slight pain.

"Lazy," my mother said.

The colors cleared and she was standing over me, frowning. "Stop staring into space," she yelled. "Get out there and do something."

What she meant was do something gorgeous with your life. "Work," she said, and Latin and Greek, and math to master my wandering mind, hers was a household of dream and muscle both.

I went into the woods a lot that summer. The woods were cool, and I could close my eyes, and if colors came when the birds cooed or the oak trees creaked, I didn't have to worry; I could drift. And if the colors didn't come, and the world smelled only of itself, then I could play. I found toads in those woods, and Indian arrowheads. I cut a worm in half and made two worms. I got blood beneath my fingernails and bird dirt on my palms.

"You," she said, when I came home one day, "are filthy."

She slapped me, hard, across the cheek.

I hate to say it, but it's true.

My cheek.

And then, she reached across the piano keys, a longing in her look now, and smudged her pinkie to my soiled face.

Looked at the dirt I'd transferred to her finger like it was chocolate. Oh, that she could sink so low. Oh, that she, like me, could sleep.

Put your finger in your mouth, Mom, go on.

This, the gift I gave her.

. . .

Even before the smells and sights and, later, the terrible slamming seizures, even before all this, my mother thought I was doomed, which, in her scheme of things, was much better than being mediocre. I was disobedient and careless, I climbed with boys, I ran with boys, and where, she wanted to know, where would this end? I would surely become a street girl, and wind up being shipped to a filthy brothel crawling with hairy tropical bugs in Buenos Aires. For my part, her predictions confused me, because they didn't seem to match the facts of my mundane life—the facts, the facts, they probe at me like the problem they are—I was, I thought, it seemed, mildly curious, fond of red-eared turtles, good at reading but bad at math, with teeth a tad bit yellow. For her part, her predictions seemed to excite her, because when she spoke of them her words had a certain slinky sound, a lush quality to the consonants, *filthy* she would say like a hungry person pronounces *chocolate*, *brothel* she would say, like, well, like someone longing for and scared of sex.

. . .

I wanted to get my mother a gift. I scratched at the ground with sticks, split the milkweed pods. Not this, no. Not that, no. I went to the store in town—Accents Unlimited—and roamed amongst vanilla-scented candles, heart-shaped pillows, but I knew none of it would do.

The year I turned ten, the year of what I called my colored hearing and my smells, my father gave her his surprise. I think he loved her, or, like me, her unhappiness was his. He partnered up with Irving Busney in the bakery business, and now we had toppling apple muffins in the mornings and a double salary from a double job—prayer man and business man—and so he announced a vacation.

We went to Barbados. We flew. We flew! I had never been on a plane before. I loved the bubble windows, and the stewardesses who wore wings on their busts.

I loved Logan Airport, in Boston, from which we departed on a snowy day, a typical New England winter day when the trees were in ice and the old slush stank and everyone was grumpy. We left early in the morning, when the air was blue and only a few lights flickered in our neighbors' windows. We were extremely excited. On the island, we were going to stay in a place called the Princess Hotel. My mother had brought me to Decelles the week before, and the saleslady took us to the Winter Cruise Section, and I got to buy a bikini with dots on it. I got sandles with turquoise stones studded along them. I got white gloves—*for dinners*, my mother said—and crisp white dresses and also shorts.

And we left Boston on a snowy dawn, dark airport, smell of grime and fuel, and I drank chocolate milk as the plane went up. And a wonderful, ecstatic feeling came over me, a feeling which I attributed to the plane, but which I now know happens to some epileptics when the altitude changes, like you are getting closer to God, and gold, and sweet and smells, and I saw the sun rising in the sky from a whole new vantage point. The tawny sun rose like a lazy lion, all hot fur in a pink safari sky. The plane roared, and then was quiet, and I said to my father, "Are we flying?"

And then we landed, and just like that the world was different. The ecstasy passed. Fear came, a distinct sense that something horrible would happen soon. A stewardess leaned close and said, "It's not the jungle here, you know, it's a lovely island," and I said, "Yes," but the fear, which I now know, like the ecstasy, is also a part of the preseizure state, wouldn't pass.

We went down the plane's steep stairs. "Please, God," I was saying to myself, "please, God, let her like this." If you had asked me then just why I was afraid, I would have told you, *My mother my mother please let her be pleased my mother.* I would not have told you about the epileptic's electrical arousal in the brain's emotional centers, how the fear and joy, the intense prismatic sharpness of things, all come from something as small as a single cortical spark. That was not my story then, and it is not my story now, although it is the right story, the true story, not my mother but matter more basic still; or is it?

Here's what was true. Barbados. Palm trees with leaky coconuts, the humid wind that blew in our faces as we walked across the runway. There were a lot of black people, and no snow. Outrageous flowers, redder than crayons, waved in the wind. A cab took us to our hotel. The Princess Hotel. Would this, finally, be what it was she wanted?

. . .

What we did. Deep-sea fishing on a glass-bottomed boat. Caves, where Basien bats hung upside down. Piña coladas, plums in sauce, raw sugar sucked straight from the cane. This is what I remember best about Barbados. The sugarcane. Everywhere we drove there were fields and fields of it, stalks harvested under hot sun by men with small machetes. Chop chop. Castles of sugar and sweat. The sun always shone, except for the squalls that scrabbled across the sky, opened up on us, and then departed, leaving the sugar mounds damp and pooled in places. I loved those hills of sugar. There, the fear went away. Wet from the ocean, wet from sweat, I rolled in the mounds and came to her like candy.

I watched her. *Please please let her be pleased.* When the captain pointed out the coral, I looked for the movements of pleasure in her mouth, but found none. I watched her like I should have watched my sinking sickening self. I watched her like I now, an amateur gardener, watch the weather when it might be bad. Clear sky, clouds to the left? Force of the wind? Bring in the seedlings? Sudden frost? Rising heat? What?

. . .

Here were my clues. Her postcards home. She bought postcards every day and scripted out messages, her handwriting a series of careful curves. "Lovely time," she wrote to a woman named Nance. "Dear Nance, lovely time. Lovely island. We're purchasing a second home here." Or, "Emma, I'm painting every day, the colors are magnificent." And yet, I'd never seen her paint, and I'd heard nothing of a second home, but then again, what did I know? Did she paint in private? Was there a second home my parents might reveal to me? It could have all been fact. It could have all been fiction. I looked at the names on my mother's postcards—Nance, Emma, Shelly, Judith, Lil, and said those names over and over to myself, like a song. Like words might make it real.

We were to leave the island on New Year's Day. We were to celebrate on New Year's Eve, at the hotel, where the chefs were putting on quite a feast. Three whole days before the New Year's Eve feast, management posted the menu in all the prominent places, appetizers, sherbet to clear the palate, crusty rolls, and the main course, lobster.

My father said, "I think that's going too far, Anita."

She said, "We never keep kosher outside the house. We haven't kept kosher the whole time we've been here."

"But shellfish," my father said.

"A fish with a shell," she said. "It's no different than fish without a shell, which God knows we eat enough of."

"I don't like it," he said, but you could tell, anyone could tell, he didn't know how to stand up to her. I hate to say it, it's so politically incorrect, but I think if he'd been brutish, my father, she may have learned to love him.

"Lobster," she went around saying. "Have you ever had lobster? Dipped in butter?"

She said it while staring up at my father, daring him to leap into the ring with her, but he wouldn't. He had fair skin, freckled everywhere, and he spent a lot of time in the hotel, where the air conditioners shuddered and the sun came through the slats in bright chinks.

The morning of the feast I woke early. I often did. I liked the sugar hills best at dawn. This particular morning, though, I stopped by my parents' hotel room door. There were no sounds coming from the room, so I don't know why I was drawn. I never went into their bedroom at home without permission. Perhaps, here, it was the quality of the silence, silence as sharp as a shout. Their room was connected to mine, and so they hadn't locked up. I turned the handle.

It was early, maybe 6:00 A.M. They were lying on their separate sides of the bed. My mother was curled on her side, my father on his back in boxer shorts. What was it that gave this moment its particular horror for me? They were two people in bed, bored in bed, hardly a tragedy, nothing like Northern Ireland, or Panama. But I froze. I saw the spongy pouf of my father's stomach, my mother's arms where the blue veins had an ethereal glow. The room was still dawn-dark, and bottles of gin stood sweating in the cooler. The room, despite her perfumes, had a sour smell, and the air-conditioning unit banged above them. The heavy hotel curtains moved in the false breeze. Slowly, my mother turned, opened her eyes. She seemed to be entirely awake, as though she'd been waiting for me. She seemed monstrous. She did not say a word. Just saw me standing there and stared, and stared, as if to say, "So now you see," and I, well, I stepped back.

. . .

We didn't have our lobster. It required bibs and tongs, scraping green gunk from dark places, and my mother, it turned out, couldn't lower herself to partake. I could tell she wanted to, though, the same way I could tell she secretly longed to walk with me in the woods, to take in soil, to sleep the heavy, sweaty sleep of the rude and the relaxed. Instead she watched from the polite sidelines as men and women at other tables cracked open the casing and speared the white meat, holding it up like a tiny trophy before popping it in their mouths.

No, in the end, my mother couldn't allow herself that lobster. We ate chicken instead. There was dancing and colored lights in all the trees, and the patio stones were freshly washed. And maybe because it was the New Year, my brain gave me not only jasmine that night but many other wonderful nameless odors, so strong I felt sick in a sweet way.

There was liquor galore. My mother had a thirst, she drank and drank. The pianist played many lovely songs, and she, elegant, waltzed from table to table, making comments. "His pianissimo's a little off," she said a little too loudly.

"He doesn't have much Mozart in him," she announced at the end of an aria.

"Anita, be quiet," my father hissed, a chicken bone in his mouth.

I, for my part, was mortified, because she was such a big woman with a big voice, and everyone on the patio could hear her.

Including the poor pianist.

"Play 'Gay Tarantella,' " she shouted out.

He did and when it was over she sighed and said, "Such heavy hands."

A few people tittered.

"Music," my mother announced to the patio, "is a delicate art form. It should breathe."

"Anita, we're going," my father said, spitting out his chicken bone.

Everyone was listening.

"Do you play, ma'am?" the pianist said, glaring at her. "Perhaps you could do a better job?"

"Do I play?" she said, laughing. "What a sweet question. You are a sweet," she said to the musician, who, by the by, was black. "You are a sweet man with many sweet things in you, but with no thunder. A man should have thunder," she said, glancing at my father.

"Do you play, ma'am?" the pianist said again. He was still glaring. "Would you like to play some thunder for the crowd?"

All the waiters had stopped, and all the people had stopped eating, and the patio looked like a frozen place, a garish game of freeze tag.

"I have my own Steinway at home," she said.

"How nice," the pianist said.

"And I've played," she said, and paused. "I've played in . . . many situations."

"Do take a seat," he said, standing up from the bench and gesturing to his place.

And then she went forward. I stopped being mortified and started being proud. Or, I was proud and mortified both, and my own dizziness was getting worse. She had balls, and she had vodka. She never stumbled or slurred, though: You could only tell if you knew her, from the metal smell of her breath.

She pushed out the seat and sat down to take it. She made a big show of positioning her hands and straightening her shoulders, just like she had practiced all those hours at home. The party waited, waited for a symphony. Waited for the maestro she'd claimed herself to be. I know I could not have seen her face—her back was to me—but I have such a clear memory, a clear dream of my mother's face as she sat at the peak of a promise she'd made, stuck in a lie, three blind mice all she knew. *Just play it, Mom,* I thought. *Three blind mice, see how they run, just play it and get it over with.* I think she stared down at the ivory keys, the bared teeth, and all things sober passed across her face, because she did not know. She must have known she did not know. Somewhere in the world, if you pressed the right keys, or the right combination of keys, there would be thunder and Mozart, and more; there would be all you'd craved but been too clenched to take, soft songs you could sleep to, chords like a hammock, maybe, and a hand to hold, the way time slows in a tub. If you knew the right notes. Which she didn't.

You could've heard a pin drop. You could've heard the petals fall from a flower while we waited, and waited. Her hands poised over the keys. Sobering up. "I suppose not," she finally said, and stood, and carefully, carefully walked away.

That night, I had my first seizure.

. . .

At the school where I later went to learn about my illness, I saw movies, so I know what it is; it is not careful. You grit your teeth, you clench, a spastic look crawls across your face, your legs thrash like a funky machine, you hit hard and spew, you grind your teeth with such a force you might wake up with a mouth full of molar dust, tooth ash, the residue of words you've never spoken, but should have. You bite your mouth—I do at least—chew it to pieces from the inside out, a mythical hunger, my whole self jammed into my jaw.

When I woke up my father was bending over me and then a doctor came, a guest of the hotel. He did not seem impressed. "Seizure," he pronounced. "Rather common in young ones," and then he left.

I can dimly recall seeing my father's face in the background of the hotel room, pale and shocked. My mother, as it turns out, missed that first seizure. She had fallen into one of her restless sleeps, a sleep so fractured and tentative she always had a veil of exhaustion in her glittery eyes. Sometime during the night my father must have told her; he must have woken her and said, "She's had a seizure," and so I waited, but she never appeared to nurse me that night, and this is a grudge I still hold.

We flew back to Boston the next day. How did I feel? Shrinks have been asking me that question for decades now, as though the origin of whatever mental miseries I might have are linked to that first fall down. How did I feel, the shrinks ask, and offer me some Dilantin; you must be depressed, the shrinks say, and proffer me some Prozac. How did I feel? I'll tell you. We were in a plane, going backward. Before, I had watched the tawny sun lionize the sky, and now, through the Boeing's bubble windows, I watched it set; I watched it soil the sky and burn up a bird and take every cloud and taint it. We zoomed through the air, held up by nothing but hope, and at any moment, I knew, we could crash.

Also, my head throbbed. Someone was playing the piano in my head, and the wooden notes kept bonging my brain.

I puked in a bag and that gave me some relief.

My mother must have heard me puking, and said, from the seat in front of me, "Just give the waste to the stewardess, Lauren."

We landed in the dark. We took a taxi home in the dark.

That night, finally, she came to me. She stood over me in my bed for a while, and she seemed entranced. Or maybe it was I who was entranced. No, I think it was her, actually. She stood over me, her eyes roving me from head to foot—this daughter of hers, this grand mal, this big badness—and then, finally, she touched my head like it was hot.

. . .

In Beth Israel Hospital, where my mother took me the next day, I sat in a small room and drew clocks, and houses, and put together red cubes to make red-and-white patterns. "What happened?" my pediatrician, Dr. Patterson, asked.

"I smelled something funny," I said. "I remember, before I fell, I smelled a funny thing."

"What was it?" he said.

I searched for the words. Now I know that, prior to seizures, in states called auras, people frequently smell strange things. I've been in seizure support groups and heard the wackiest olfactory tales, the woman who was hounded by the smell of charred steak, another by the odor of a past lover's shampoo. The smells live, and though doctors claim they are purely physiological phenomena, without mental meaning, I cannot help but think the smells have significance; we smell what we want, or cannot allow ourselves to want; we smell our own stink, we smell our sin, we smell the tang of an unspoken hope.

"Lobster," I said.

"You smelled lobster," the doctor repeated, writing it down.

"Lobster?" my mother said. She raised an eyebrow. She was holding her square purse to her chest.

"Yes," I said. "I smelled the lobster. I smelled salty lobster and butter."

"Lobster and butter, what a meal that would've been," my mother said.

The doctor looked up, confused. "Excuse me?" he said.

I giggled.

"And the green gunk too, I smelled that."

"That's enough, Lauren," my mother said. "You're losing your credibility."

But she had a small smile on her face, and, well, just for the sake of the story let's say she even licked her lips a little bit, and that was the first time I realized how, through illness, I might be able to give her good food.

. . .

There were a lot of tests—the Wada Test, the Ray Figure Drawing Test, the Wechsler Memory Scales Test, the Digit Span Test. I took an IQ test, where, according to my mother, I scored in the genius range, but we all know she never told the truth. I had an electroencephalogram, little suckers hooked up to my head and my brain waves rolling out of a machine like a receipt from a cash register. Ribbons and ribbons of brain waves, and later, when the doctor showed them to us, we could see, my mother and I, how in some places the waves were smooth, but in others, spiky as stiletto heels, and in still others, a series of rapid round *u*'s, like this—*UUUUUUUUU*—a language gone awry.

"She has epilepsy," I heard her whisper to someone on the phone, Nance, maybe, or Emma. "She has epilepsy, but so did van Gogh, you know."

She asked for a clipping of my brain waves and took them home, and a change came over her. She seemed to almost like the illness. She seemed disgusted, which I would have expected, but then a moment later, I saw her looking at me with wishes in her eyes, as though she, too, might like to drop and thrash, to break the brittle caul of cleanliness and artifice.

"Will, Lauren," she said to me, "use your will to get you out of this." She practiced the piano and, even with my seizures, took me skating so I could be a skating star. One morning, though, before we dressed to go out to the pond, I saw her tracing my brain's undulations, those sleepy dips, those troughs filled with earth and snooze, sex and spasm, and I'd say she smiled then.

"You," she said to me, all sternness, "need to learn to pull yourself together."

But she touched my head gently now, like it was hot, like it was cold, like it was warm, like it was whatever she was not, a wild and totally true world in there, a place she had forsaken for artifice, etiquette, marriage, mediocre love, and which I had returned to her; here, Mom; have my head.

. . .

She was right. A lot of famous people have had epilepsy. Take Dostoevski, for instance. He had a serious case of it. Saint Paul probably had epilepsy, and from its craziness he crafted a world religion. Van Gogh, of course, had epilepsy, which may be why he is the van Gogh we know, a painter of tilted stars, low-hanging moons, fields full of flowers and blue vortexes that take all sensible shape away. If you look at a van Gogh painting, you might get a sense of what the world looks like as you go down. In the weeks that followed, it kept happening to me. I was a wrong girl, I flamencoed on the floor, feathers came out of my ears, and my body made music, made thunder and sleep, made Mozart, my hands curled into lobster claws.

Epilepsy shoots your memory to hell, so take what I say, or don't. This I think I recall. One week after Barbados, after her failed music, the vodka, her empty eyes in the hotel room, I woke from a long seizure on the floor. Every muscle ached. There was blood in my mouth. I opened my eyes and saw her standing above me, staring at me, probably, for a long long time, as just a few days earlier, in the Basien dawn, I had stared at her. I had looked into that hotel room and seen how all her energy was really deadness; not me. I was a girl in motion. I was wrong and dark and full of smells. When a seizure rolled through me, it didn't feel like mine; it felt like hers—her ramrod body sweetening into spasm. She gave it all to me, and I returned it all to her, this wild, rollicking, hopeful life, this Chuck Berry blast, all striving sunk to the bottom of the brain's deep sea; crack a claw, Mom.

Rest with me when it's over.

This, the gift I gave you.

How we held each other.

PART TWO

THE RIGID

STAGE

CHAPTER 3

LEARNING TO FALL

My mother believed that will, not love, was what made the world go round, and I agreed. I was a wrong girl but I had always worked hard at what I did. I owned a pair of skates, nubby tights, and a white muff made from real rabbit fur. I had gotten my ears pierced when I was only eight years old, and all dressed up in my skating outfit, I looked like a holiday.

Before and at first even after my seizures started, I skated at a pond. For years my mother had been buying me books about champions, the biographies of Dorothy Hamill and Estelle Drier. At home my shelves were stocked full of fame, and when it came to the ice, my mother thought I had potential.

Skating is a sport of bones and grace, a sport where you fly on water like a prophet but fall, sphincter first, on the solidest surface. It hurts and you have to push yourself. You have to push yourself first to go out in the cold, and then to walk over a place where, right beneath, sharks and whales are waiting for you, and then to leap against your better judgment, when your whole self is longing just to nap. The place was called Dehaney's Pond, and it was always beautiful in a winter way. Each December, January, February, reeds crackling like whiskers in the winter wind. "Spin," she would shout, and I did it. The more it hurt, the better I was. "Leap now," she would shout, "with your toe turned out," and I did it, even when my lungs burned and my lips lost all their moisture; I did it until I went far away, far, far away to someplace silver, and beyond pain.

Will is what makes the world go round. If you want something, push, pull, shake and scrape until it forms. The same holds true for the soul. The soul is a pile of moist manure, and only by tilling and shoveling might you turn it into gold. The work was hard, hard! But the possibilities— limitless, a fairy-tale world where you could endlessly become.

I worked. For my whole life, in sickness and in health, I had worked at being bad and good and strong. I was my mother's girl. Before the epilepsy came on hard, I skated, and I had my own private sports as well. "The Jews," my mother liked to say proudly, "marched forty miles in the snow without shoes." When I was very little, maybe six or seven, I had taken to marching around our yard, barefoot in the snow, for no other reason than it was just the way to live. Either you did it or you died.

Once, when marching, I had seen a cardinal. He was Chinese red, and he kept staring at me. "Three steps more," the cardinal had said, and so I went three steps more. That bird got in my blood and ordered me around. "Three steps more," he said, and the next day four steps, and sometimes I longed to let the cardinal go, to open my heart and have him soar out, but I couldn't. Instead I went three steps, then four, then five, all for fear and maybe a little love.

But after the epilepsy began, and then got worse, the skating stopped. This is how it happened. I had my first seizure in Barbados, my second one in our kitchen back in Boston. And then, the winter of my tenth year, I started to seize a few times a week or even once a day. Still, I did my glides and my bends, until the January morning, just at dawn, when my mother took me to the pond for practice. I clumped out over the ice in my skates, pushed off, and started my moves. I remember the day was warmish, with a little slick of sweat over the ice, and the reeds had thawed so their boggy smell came out. "Pivot and turn," my mother shouted, and as I did, as I entered the thawing air, a memory suddenly came to me, a memory so clear and absolute it must have been engraved in the back rooms of my brain for a long time, and I was finding it just now, perfect and whole. A memory that was moving slowly even while I spun fast, even while I felt my legs get big, get bloated, and my hands— huge now—filled with helium. *Help me,* I thought, and that was when I recalled that a boy had once drowned in this pond in the summer, and I'd heard about how they'd dragged for the body, his limbs all swollen and soft. *Help me,* I thought, and the smell came, bad, like a sewer when it's open, and at the same time an exquisite sense of pleasure, of trumpet, I couldn't breathe. I came down out of the sky. I think I came down fast, and a little chicken was running around, Chicken Little! Chicken Little!—and then the sky was falling on me as I sank below the surface of the pond and I saw the boy down there in the murk. "Help me," I wanted to say, but in water there is no voice; there is no speed; there is just a terribly slow suck.

When I woke up, I was in the hospital, but I didn't know that right away because my head hurt so much. "Did I drown?" I asked.

"No," the nurse said. "But you've had another seizure."

Apparently, then, the ice hadn't broken.

I lay there for a while in the monstrous bed. The sheets were made of meringue; they crackled whenever I moved. I stopped moving. I closed my eyes. I knew, even before the doctor told us, that this was the worst seizure I'd had so far. "I didn't die; I didn't die; I didn't die," I kept saying to myself.

The doctor came into the room. It was Dr. Patterson, my pediatrician. I liked him, even though his stethoscope was always cold.

"Am I going to die?" I said to Dr. Patterson.

He came over to my bed. He looked down at me. Then he smiled, took out his stethoscope, and put it on my nose. "I don't think so," he said, listening to my nose. "I think you'll be just fine."

How could I believe that, though, when Chicken Little, who was supposed to be a silly chicken all in a dither, was really right? I was learning, now, that at any minute I could go in a dangerous way. I was not a girl at all, but a marionette, and some huge hand—my mother's hand?—held me up, and for a reason I absolutely could not predict, that hand might let the strings go slack, oh, God.

My mother came into the room. Dr. Patterson said to her, "Just a little sprain in the wrist, a few bruises. But this seizure was more serious than the others. I can't emphasize enough how important the phenobarbital is going to be. She needs a very high dose, six hundred milligrams."

My mother nodded, but she didn't like the idea of drugs at all.

"And," Dr. Patterson said, "I think, as we discussed before, she should go to Saint Christopher's for a stint."

They had told me about Saint Christopher's. It was a special school in Topeka, Kansas. The doctors wanted me to go to Topeka, Kansas, where Dorothy and her little dog had danced off the earth and fallen into a land of lemon drops and witches. They wanted me to go and board there at the special school funded by the Epilepsy Society, so I could get a physical education, and learn to fall the right way, and not break my bones, and it would all take only a month.

"That school," my mother said, "is run by nuns."

It was night. I was back at home, listening through the toilet bowl as my parents discussed the pros and cons.

"Agreed," my father said. "That's a problem."

"And many of the children who go there," my mother said, "are Down's."

I didn't know what *downs* meant. I pictured goose feathers, fairy children as delicate as feathers all dropping from the sky and blown around.

"Then maybe we really should increase the drug," my father said.

But my mother didn't want to increase the drug because a high dose of phenobarbital gave me a rash all over, a rash so persistent I even got little red bumps along my lower eyelids and in my vag too. *Vag* was the word I used, my own private word for *vagina.* Even back then I had private words, places apart from my mother. There was my vag, which now had bumps in it, there was my earlobe, which I liked to touch, there were the woods, where the trees arched and dripped. Sometimes I wanted to go and live in a place apart forever, a place where I could roll around in the dirt and lick things.

And so at night, when I was alone, I took to touching my vag bumps, running my fingers over them lightly so the pain was just the merest shiver, the air on the rash like a damp cloth pressed to a fevered forehead, and I would lie there night after night on the cusp of coolness and heat, and I tried to find someplace soothing.

Instead I got smaller.

I got fears.

One day, soon after the seizure on the ice, I saw *Seventeen* magazine in a store window. *Someday,* I thought to myself, *I will be seventeen, and then I will be eighteen, and then before I know it I'll be eighty,* and I got so scared by that thought I had to sit down on the curb.

I saw a hearse drive by, with blue curtains in the windows. I started to wonder if the spirits of dead people stood under trees and waited to grab at you. It was a shame to be scared of trees, those natural chuppahs, those homes in the middle of the widest world, but scared I was, and so I stood out in the unsheathed sun.

"If you pay attention," my mother said to me, leaning in close, "if you try very hard, you'll be able to stop these seizures."

I could see her face clearly at these moments, eyebrows tweezed in taut lines. My mother had a mole which she tried every day to cover with cream, but its blackness bled through, a little tip of dark, and that was the only part of her I could ever think to touch.

She read a book called *The New Cure for Epilepsy*, a book which talked about going off drugs completely and learning to breathe in a deep way.

One day we went together to a psychologist at a special epilepsy clinic called the Center for Voluntary Control over Internal Processes. We had to drive an hour to get there. We passed men in orange helmets fixing the highway. The helmets made me so sad I felt everything turn to dust in me. That's the way it was after the seizures began. Anything, at any moment, might become unbearable, might be a sign of some absurdity we would never escape. Helmets. Ponds. Trees. Pears. Just let me close my eyes.

Now I know that depression and epilepsy often go together. That's why I take Prozac now, as an adult. One of the reasons, anyway. It's a proven fact that those who have epilepsy also have a higher incidence of depression, but I wonder if the epilepsy causes the depression, or if the depression is because of the epilepsy, which is, when all is said and done, an illness so existential, so oddly spiritual, you are stuck out in the stratosphere with Sartre and Kierkegaard, with dead dogs and owls.

Dr. Swan, maybe, would help me. She had a lot of posters on the walls of the clinic, posters of mountaintops and streams with inspirational sayings on the bottom. One poster, though, really stood out. A human brain on a green stem. The brain was bumpy, like it really is, but ringed with pale petals, and in the background a sky suspiciously blue, the kind of sky they show in decongestant commercials. Underneath the stem was a poem in bold letters:

> *The Brain Is Essential to Life*
> *I Want My Brain to Act Calmly and Normally*
> *I Will Do Everything I Can to Help My Brain Act Calmly*
>   *and Normally*

"Come in," said Dr. Swan.

We went into her office.

"What are your triggers?" said Dr. Swan.

My mother and I were in the office together. It was our first session.

"Triggers?" my mother said. Both she and I had gotten all dressed up to see the special doctor, my mother in a stole made of fox fur, with a fox head biting a fox tail, and me in my white muff.

"Yes, triggers," Dr. Swan said. "Oftentimes a seizure comes after a period of stress—"

"Oh yes," my mother said, interrupting. She folded her hands in her lap. "I'm aware of that phenomenon." I could see she was going into her impress-a-person mode. "The stress hormone cortisol and all."

Dr. Swan's office was wood paneled, and Dr. Swan, I've failed to mention, looked nothing like a swan. She wore a dark serious suit, and she was old, and had her gray hair in a bun on top of her head.

"Cortisol, adrenaline," my mother said, still trying to make a splash, when, really, she'd just read this in a pamphlet yesterday.

"I said triggers," Dr. Swan repeated, her voice low and severe. She was a formidable woman and didn't like detours.

My mother stopped, snapped her mouth shut, and for just a moment she seemed flustered. Then it passed. She lowered her head like a bull lowers its horned head for the charge and said, "My daughter has no stressors. She has an exceptionally placid life."

"Mrs. Slater," Dr. Swan said, sighing. "This is not psychotherapy. I am a behaviorist. I have neither the time, nor you, I'm sure, given the cost of this treatment, the money, to dismantle your denial. Every child has stressors."

I thought, at this point, my mother would grab me and leave, but she didn't. Instead she crossed one leg over the other and said in a voice suddenly open and warm, "Dr. Swan. May I call you Emma? That might make it easier to talk."

"If you wish," said Emma.

"She did," my mother said, lowering her voice, "take a bad fall when she was three. Her father, well, it was her father who—in a rage—"

I had known nothing about this fall, and my father, who now, years later and long after their divorce, lives alone in a retirement home in Florida, says it's simply not true.

Dr. Swan must have thought so too, for she turned impatiently from my mother and looked straight at me. "Stressors?" she said, as though I were forty, not ten.

I shrugged.

Her voice softened. "Let me explain," she said, leaning across her desk toward me. "Sometimes people get nervous and upset, it's perfectly normal. In school, maybe a person gets nervous before a test. Or in families," she said, glancing back briefly at my mother, "it's all right for there to be stressors in families, and if we know about them, we can help you avoid them, and any seizures that follow."

"Thank you," I said, stupidly.

"Lauren," my mother said. She made a show of putting her hand on my knee. "We have always talked openly. Tell the doctor about your stressors. It's normal."

I looked at her. I looked at Dr. Swan. I went back and forth between them with my eyes, but with my mouth I could do nothing.

. . .

Three times a week we went, my mother always in the waiting room from that time forward. The second session she stood to come in with me, and Dr. Swan held up her hand and said, "That won't be necessary."

There, in the dark-paneled office, it was just me and the swan and the leaded-glass windows. When it snowed, the flakes through the glass looked huge and ragged and the bare branches out there were networks of nerves like the pictures I'd seen in the neurologist's office. As spring came, the nerves grew buds that did not seem beautiful to me, little green cysts with pus in them. I wanted to tell Dr. Swan about the sick trees. I wanted to tell her about the seizure on ice, and the boy I'd seen at the bottom of the pond. He'd been there, and as time went by I realized he had tried to talk to me. He had tried to touch me as I fell, reaching out a hand, a white waxy thing.

I said nothing, though. I felt to speak would be to betray my mother, especially because, at the end of every session, she grilled me about what had happened in the office, her gloved hands holding tight to the steering wheel. "Why don't you tell me about your mother?" Dr. Swan sometimes suggested, and then I wanted to let out the truth, to say, "Oh, I hate her! Oh, I love her!" Sometimes, after I'd woken up from a seizure, I felt so sorry for her. I felt it was really she who'd had the seizure, she whose muscles really ached, and over and over again in my mind, I brought my mother milk.

Dr. Swan, for her part, seemed to feel genuinely sorry for me. Every time I went in there, she had a plate of cookies on her desk. She taught me deep breathing, which my mother and I practiced three times a day at home. "Breathe!" my mother shouted, and so I did. "One one one," she told me to chant to myself at every inhalation. "One one one," I chanted, which meant you're the one, the only one, the one mom one mom one mom, until I felt I would choke.

. . .

A new desire came to me. I had never seen a real true dead person, and I decided I wanted to. We had a funeral home in our neighborhood, and so I went there when there was a funeral. The line to see the body was so long it was out the door and down the street. I stood with the other mourners and tried to look sad, but I wasn't sad. I was nothing.

I never got to see the body, though, because right there in public I had a seizure and pissed myself, and I became the body to be seen. Understand? I was ashamed.

"You should not be ashamed," my father said. "There was once a rabbi in Jerusalem," my father said, "and a sick man came to him and said, 'Rabbi, take away my stigma.'

"And the rabbi, who was a wise man, shrugged and said, 'Sickness is sickness. The sun is the sun, laughter is laughter and tears just tears. There is never a need to make more of God's world than what is.' "

My father told me this one morning, four days before winter break was to end and I was to return to school, where kids would see me different.

"Would you like an egg?" my father said.

"I don't know what the story means," I said.

"Of course you do," he said, and then I did. And I felt comfort come from a place where I had never even sought it, not from my mother, but from this man, who that morning made me an egg.

. . .

If comfort could come from him, then it must be hidden in other places too. This is what I started to realize, the wisdom that would, finally, lead me away from her. Comfort must rest within other people's palms, in their flower beds, in the saucers they keep stacked on painted kitchen shelves. The next day, my mother and I drove to the supermarket. I looked out at all the houses we passed, and I had a dream of houses. There, a blue one with a wide, pretty porch, a hammock hanging in the still air. A stone house, with tiny Christmas lights in every window. A house with a birdbath on its lawn, a house with white curtains and white steam coming from its laundry vent. Inside those houses there were girls my age, every one of them cooking eggs. They cracked egg after egg against a skillet, and ate them fried and frilly, soaked in butter, with toast their mothers had made.

I thought I might like to live in another house. I thought that in other houses girls could sleep instead of skate.

What I hadn't told her. Lately I had taken to playing a secret game, to wandering around neighborhoods and peering in whatever windows I could. If I liked what I saw, I then rang the doorbell and hid in the bushes. The best part was hiding there, seeing the door open wide, a man with rumpled hair, a sleepy-looking lady, a kid with a cup of cocoa, all opening the doors and looking around, and I, in the bushes, seeing a space I might enter.

Now, my mother and I entered the supermarket parking lot.

"Put your hat on," my mother said.

I had bruises on both sides of my face, from falling, and the hat, with its own built-in earmuffs, covered things up.

I put my hat on, but in a wrong way. She sighed, reached over, and jammed it down so hard it hurt.

"Put your Chap Stick on," my mother said. My lips were crusty, from biting them during seizures, and the ointment softened the sores and absorbed the blood.

She peered at me. Slowly she shook her head back and forth, back and forth. "Look at you," she said.

I sat very still.

"Look at you," she said again, her voice oddly quiet, disgusted, and soft in a way that scared me.

"Mom," I said.

We went in. On that particular day, there were policemen in the supermarket. Now, I have no idea why they were there. They were just hanging around, with guns on their hips.

We started our shopping. After a while, I got hot in my hat and when she wasn't looking I loosened it. My mouth ached, from chewing at it during seizures, the linings of my cheeks all ragged.

We went to the produce section, where there were many

grapefruit. Each one was pudgy and yellow on the outside, but I knew, on the inside, the sting of its secretions, the tartness in my open sores. Just looking at the grapefruit I started to feel sick.

With my head in a whirl, I reached out toward a grapefruit and began to peel it; I had no idea what I was doing.

"Lauren," my mother said, "don't *do that* to the fruit."

But there was a little motor going inside me, a key clacking in my back, and I kept on, and the swelling in my hand, and, this time, a feeling of intense fixation—*fruit fruit fruit,* I was saying to myself, and I wanted to wreck every piece of that stinging citrus stuff.

Dr. Swan, in our last session, had told my mother and me about a new trick for stopping seizures. If you recognized a seizure coming on, you were to grab the person, shake her hard by the shoulders, and scream "No!" It was called the Startle and Shake Response, and it had, supposedly, gotten some good results across the country.

"Lauren," my mother said.

I raised both my hands. Sometimes I did that just before I went. It was because my hands felt so funny, so big and drifty, I just had to raise them.

This, then, was her sign. I felt her hands lock on to my shoulders, and with all the vigor in her vigorous suppressed self, she shook me and yelled, "No! No! No!"

The good news is, it worked. Not 100 percent, but we got a fair result. I had a small seizure in the supermarket, but nothing anyone could really see.

The bad news is, the public misunderstood. My hat

had fallen off my bruised-up head, and I had bitten my lips down to blood again. Picture this: a big person shrieking at a little person, hauling her around, the little person pocked with contusions and oozing from various sensitive spots, it doesn't look good for the big one.

We were both in a daze, I think, and when we came to, the whole damn supermarket was silent and staring.

"Well," my mother said, and smoothed her hair back with the flat of her palm.

A woman with a baby in her stroller glared at us, and then walked away. I saw the butcher holding his knife. "Someone help that child," he bellowed. But no one moved.

"It's not," said my mother, "it's, people, it's not what—"
She started to cry.

"Oh, Mom," I said. "Oh, Mom."

The two policemen came forward. One knelt down by me and gently blotted my lip with his handkerchief. Right then and there I fell in love. Every button on his suit was copper, like a coin.

"Ma'am," the other one said to my mother, "ma'am, may we step aside and talk?"

We all stepped aside to talk. There are many private places in a supermarket, you would be surprised.

My prince kept his hand on my shoulder the whole time. The other one said, in the privacy, "Ma'am, we have to file on you."

"File what?" my mother said.

The policeman sighed. He looked genuinely pained. "Child abuse," he said. "It's against the law."

"You've got to be kidding me," my mother said. "I don't—"

"And, we'll have to take her with us."

"This is my daughter," my mother said, starting to shake like she was having a seizure. "This is my daughter and she's not going anywhere."

"The law states," the policeman said, "that if we deem a child to be in imminent danger, we must place her in the custody of social services."

"Oh please," my mother said. She was shaking with fear and snorting with contempt at the same time. I felt bad for her, but I also hated her snorts.

"I don't abuse my child," she said. "My child has epilepsy," she said. "Epilepsy, do you hear me? She has seizures," she said, "and that's why she looks like she does."

"Ma'am," the policeman said, "we witnessed you shaking the child, and hitting her with an open hand, and she is severely bruised."

"I never hit her with an open hand."

"Do you have epilepsy?" the princely policeman asked me.

I thought if I said yes, they would let us go. And part of me wanted us to be let go, but part of me didn't. I had had the dream of houses, the view of all the other houses I might get to live in. I knew about social services and getting put up for adoption. I'd seen Sunday's Child in the newspaper. Maybe I could be Sunday's Child, and have my picture in the paper.

"Do you have epilepsy?" he repeated.

I wanted to answer, but the words got tangled in my throat.

"Tell them, Lauren," my mother said. I heard the desperation in her voice, the fragility behind her mask of muscle, and it made me sad, so sad. I'm sorry, Mom.

And then they took me.

. . .

I went to a large brick building in the city, and a woman named Suzie Norton tried to interest me in Monopoly. I didn't want to play Monopoly. *I'm sorry, Mom,* I kept saying inside my head, but then I also had this little odd feeling of excitement, like there was mourning and happiness both.

"I could maybe go home with the policeman," I said to Suzie Norton. "The one with the black hair."

She left the room. A long time passed, and the day grew dark. The taillights of cars burned in the blue darkness, and the horns honked. Rush hour. Winter dusk. A time of black cats and sad poems. I started to cry.

The door opened. "There's been a misunderstanding," I heard someone whisper in the hall. "She does have epilepsy. We've done a home visit. There's no violations that we could find."

Suzie Norton then drove me back from where I came, from where I would probably always have to come. Her car smelled like cigarette smoke and strawberry lip gloss. She played golden oldies on the radio as we sped through town, down highways, up hills, cresting and cruising, for a little while free, *chitty chitty bang bang,* I was saying to myself, and I saw us up in the air, driving between the stars, jumping over the moon and the ocean, to Spain, maybe, or to Jupiter, where there was a different world.

. . .

That episode did change my world, and my mother's too. No more Dr. Swan. Good-bye, Dr. Swan. A high dose of drugs. Hello, drugs. And the school for falling children, in Topeka, Kansas, where Dorothy and her little dog had once lived.

"I don't," I heard my mother say to Dr. Swan on the phone, "I don't want to do the, the Startle and Shake Intervention anymore. Anymore!" she said, and hung up.

The days following the supermarket incident, she was in a rage. She was in a state. She paced the floors. She practically forced the phenobarbital into my mouth, saying, "Swallow, Lauren. I said swallow!"

I understood that I had betrayed her, and while I felt guilt, I also saw it was possible to betray her. After all, she was still standing. So was I, for that matter.

Those days, I cried easily and a lot. My skin felt tender to the touch.

For one month I would go to the special school. I got my own personal steamer trunk, with drawers and a little closet in it. I loved that steamer trunk; I loved it even through the depression, because it was a dollhouse, a box full of rooms and niches. My mother washed all my socks, and we put them in the top drawer, where they looked like rabbits resting.

"Here," she said, the morning I was to leave. She handed me a clay owl, small enough to tuck in my palm.

It seemed an odd gift. The owl had no purpose that I could understand. But when I folded my fist around the bird, the clay felt warm, the grooves suggesting feathers, suggesting flight.

My mother's eyes were rimmed with red, her face haggard.

"I love you, Mom," I said.

She nodded with her lips clamped, and then a little cry came out of her throat; she turned away.

Later on, when I was seated on the plane, I took the owl out from my pocket. I touched him, and then, like a little girl, I put him in my mouth.

. . .

Saint Christopher is the patron saint of epileptics. His statue stood in the front foyer of the convent, a dark foyer with pictures of holy people on every wall, pictures I, a Jewish girl, had never seen before. The images fascinated me. I saw angels with wings as big as monarch butterflies'; I saw a lady in blue, her robes billowing in a biblical wind. I met Christ himself, for the first time, and if I tell you I saw myself in him, would you believe me? Jesus stood at the end of a long clean hallway, perched on a marble pedestal. His limbs hung limply from his wooden cross, suggesting, to me, the sleepiness that follows seizures. His eyes half closed, a mouth as bright as a tulip, as bright as blood; I knew what he'd done, bitten his lips in pain. I loved his heart, how he made it so available. There it was, a valentine on his bony ribs, a little love message with maybe words on the underside: *Be Mine*.

The nuns were our teachers for the month. They were not our physical therapists; we had specially trained people to do that, but the nuns took us into classes and taught us all about our disease. "Julius Caesar!" Mother Fernanda wrote in bold letters on the board. "Napoleon Bonaparte!"

They told us all the famous people who had had epilepsy, and then we had to memorize the names. The nuns themselves thought memorization very important. They had rules and expectations. Whenever they passed one another in the hall, their hands folded inside their habits, they gave a graceful bow that was wonderful to watch. I heard them chanting prayers every evening at four, and every day at dawn, before the sun had risen. I opened my eyes in my bed then, in the convent dormitory, and listened to their disciplined voices float across the snowy field, and into the windows of the room where we lay.

There were fifty children altogether at the school, and ten in my dormitory. We were on a strict schedule, cooking class, sewing class, Living with Illness Discussion Group. We were up at six and in bed by eight, and so busy all the time I hardly had a moment to miss my home. It was a grueling education, but it made me muscular in a new way. I learned things my mother never would have thought to teach me, like how to wash a floor on my knees, I could do it. I learned how to scrape paint, sand wood, fix a faucet, and bake bread from scratch, pummeling the dough with my fists and then setting it to rise in its yeasty smell. I learned to milk a cow, squeezing its teats and stopping to rest, scratching the beast on its barn-warm haunches. I wired my own lamp that I made from a bottle, and when I plugged it in, it glowed, because of me. The nuns were proper, yes, proper like my mother, but also tough and handy. They hired no plumbers, no electricians, no cleaning ladies to do it for them. "You do it for yourself," they'd say, "and for the love of God."

There was one nun whom I never saw in daylight, but whom I came to love. She was the nun who carried the candle and the basin of holy water, and every evening, after lights out, she came to us. Sister Mary. She was old, and hunched up, and she carried her basin from bed to bed, so any child who wanted to be blessed could be blessed. I had received strict instructions from both my parents not to partake in anything Christian, but I wished I could. The holy water smelled perfumed, and Sister Mary, if you wanted, would dab it on your forehead and say, "You are a sweet thing."

I would never let her do it to me, because I was a Jewish girl, but she touched me anyway, on my cheek, my throat, where the little throb of sadness lived, on my forehead where the band of fear cinched tight. "You are a sweet," she'd say to me, "God's girl," and it was to those words I fell asleep.

. . .

The whole point of the school was falling, not nuns. When we weren't in classes with them, we were in the gym with the physical therapists. Epilepsy is a dangerous disease because you can hurt yourself crashing down, and so you

have to learn the right way to crash. The physical therapists started us in water. We stepped into a warm, heavily
chlorinated pool, and we learned to let ourselves go in that,
drifting backward, our hair coming out as kelp around our
heads. I watched the other girls in their bathing suits in the
water; I watched them stand in the water up to their waists,
and then topple backward, and then the lovely squelching
sound when they hit. With their eyes closed, they drifted on
their backs, and if they were twelve or older their nipples
pushed out from beneath their suits, lilies those girls, every
one.

I was a lily too. I could fall in water. The pool was warm
and I angled back into its embrace, into the brine of a body,
her body, mother. I could go there.

Two weeks into our training the physical therapists
moved us onto land. Now, years later, I can see the sense in
all this, how evolutionarily correct it all was, how they were
teaching us much more than falling; they were teaching us
living. From fish to amphibian, from flippers to feet, we
walked onto mats and the therapists said, "Take a deep
breath and let yourself go."

Have you, I want to know, ever looked at the ground as a
crash site? Try it now. Look down from the couch or chair
where you're sitting. See the sheen of wood, hear the sharp
smack of the skull as it hits. That's what we were supposed
to do.

I couldn't.

Day after day the other kids learned. They let themselves

loose and went flopping and survived it all to stand. I, however, was not that kind of girl. And no matter what the nuns
said to me about how it was all right to let yourself go, I
knew they didn't think so. They were, day after day, stern
and white, upright angels. They bowed with beauty and
never tripped. They floated on their feet and slept, so they
said, flat on their backs, with their hands folded on top of
their chests, so if the Holy Ghost should see fit to take them
in the night, they would be ready for their maker. How was
I to fall in a world like this? When I looked at the nuns,
Mother Fernanda, Sister Agnes, young nuns, pretty nuns, I
saw the skater in me. I saw how I had once leapt off the pond
in a silver swirl, and everything was elegant. I saw my
mother on the shoreline, clapping and clapping, my mother.
I had marched in the snow without shoes, and it was will that
made the world go round, right?

Right?

"Will you fall today?" the physical therapists said to me.
"Lauren, will you fall?"

I did everything I could to be good. I baked bread,
scoured the floors, memorized the names of famous epileptics. "Julius Caesar. Napoleon Bonaparte. Georg Friedrich
Handel." I could learn it all except for falling, because I was
a marionette, and even hundreds of miles away, it was her
huge hand that held me up.

At night, lying in my dorm bed, after the holy water and
the evening prayers, I took the owl out. He had yellow eyes,
and I soon discovered they glowed in the dark. In the dark

my mother's owl watched me, its shining eyes, the rustle of
its feathers as it said, *Fly.*

. . .

I think you can hold out for only so long. I think secretly
each and every one of us longs to fall, and knows in a deep
wise place in our brains that surrender is the means by which
we gain, not lose, our lives. We know this, and that is why we
have bad backs and pulled necks and throbbing pain between
our shoulder blades. We want to go down, and it hurts to
fight the force of gravity.

One day there was a serious snowstorm. The wind blew
hard. Cobras of snow swirled off the ground and flakes as
big as hunks of torn-up bread came straight out of the sky.
It was Sunday, the Christian Sabbath, and the nuns had gone
to pray. The snow smothered their voices, so I couldn't hear
the chanting, or the melodies. I watched for them out the
window. Soon, I knew, the doors of the church across the
field would open, and they would file out one by one, and
march across the white expanse to dinner.

In the distance, a radio tower light blinked. A plow with
chains on its wheels crawled through the thickness.

And then the red church doors opened and the nuns
moved across the field toward me, and it took my breath
away. I was only ten, but I knew beauty. Children do, you
know. The nuns lifted their legs high in the drifts, and their
white habits were a part of the weather, blowing around. A
catch in my throat. A tip.

Sister Maria was the first to tip. It must have been the wind. Down, down she went, and I heard an "oh my goodness," and saw a cluster of nuns come to help her up, and she stood up, laughing, shaking the snow from her folds.

And then, just like that, still laughing, maybe giddy on the excess of weather, Sister Maria pushed at Sister Agnes, who in turn threw a scoop of snow at Sister Katherine, and in the snap of some of the strangest seconds I've ever seen, this holy place became a beach party, a white-water fight, waves of snow hurled left and right, and habits flapping, and laughter, and laughter, and laughter, it caught, was fire, and I felt the glow in my chest, like my heart was Jesus' heart on the outside of my skin. I sprinted out the door and whooped with delight, it was war, it was peace, it was wet, it was warm, I pranced with the silly nuns, and to this day I don't know which sister it was who pushed me down, but down I went, the holy hand moving me down, falling onto ground, and all the snow was singing.

. . .

And so it was that I learned how to fall. The next day, and the next, and the next, I did it in class, for my physical therapist, who was so surprised and pleased she hugged me. I learned to buckle my knees and let myself loose, slipping southward, away from her, betraying her, yes, I did it, all my muscles slack.

. . .

You've probably heard of him, William James, brother of Henry, the Victorian novelist. Anyway, William was not a novelist but a philosopher who, in my opinion, had some things to say. I love it most when he writes about will. Years later, years and years after the falling school, when I had long moved on from the nuns, and my mother, and my illness itself, I read a book by William James, and, like any good book, it did not teach me something new, but drew out the wisdom that was already there, inside me.

William talks about there being two kinds of will. Will A and Will B, I call it. Will A is what we all learn, the hold your head high, stuff it down, swallow your sobs, work hard kind of will. Will B, while it seems a slacker thing, is actually harder to have. It's a *willingness* instead of a willfulness, an ability to take life on life's terms as opposed to putting up a big fight. It's about being bendable, not brittle, a person who is brave enough to try to ride the waves instead of trying to stop them. Will B is what you need in order to learn to fall. It's the kind of will my mother never taught me, and yours probably never taught you either. It's a secret greater than sex; it's a spiritual thing. Will B is not passive. It means an active acceptance, a *say yes*, and you have to have a voice and courage if you want to learn it.

If you know Will B, you know your life.

You know what my mother never learned. That it is only by entering emptiness and ugliness, not by covering it up with feathers and sprays, that you find a balance so true, no one can take it away.

Sometimes you can crack open a cliché and find a lot of truth. If you don't understand what I mean, think of the phrases *ride the wave, harness the energy of your opponent.*

Epilepsy is energy. It's a windstorm in the brain. I had that kind of energy when I left for Saint Christopher's, but when I came back home, I was a different sort of girl. I still had epilepsy, but my energy was Eastern; it was the blue petal in the inner chambers of the flame, it was hot, but it bent to the shape of the breeze blowing through.

...

My father picked me up at the airport. I had been away only one month, but a century had passed for me. This, this is a happy part of the story. In my new millennium I walked with my head held a little higher. At home that first night, I showed my parents what I'd learned at Saint Christopher's, how I could fix the dripping kitchen sink—so easy, really— a few twists and snaps of the silver spout, a tightening of the washer, there. It didn't drip after that. It flowed, when we wanted it to.

"That's quite something for a ten-year-old," my father said.

"All that money and she comes home a plumber?" my mother said, but I could tell she was impressed. I showed her how to shine the tiles on the kitchen floor with a secret solution of lemon juice and oil; I showed her how I had learned to plait my hair in fourteen seconds flat, and when we went to the hardware store I entered into an impressive discourse with the salesman on the relative merits of eyebolts versus snag hooks.

"How did you get to be so smart?" the salesman said. He tousled my hair. Now that I knew how to fall the right way,

I didn't bruise so much anymore; the purple splotches had been sucked back into my body, and I looked clean and white, well kept and hardy.

My mother smiled, but it was in a weary way.

I liked to fall. It gave me so much confidence, so much pride. I was good at it, and I knew, even though I never could have said it, that the falling skill was widely generalizable, that I would be able to use it for years to come, use it in love, use it in fear, use it in hope. I became, even, a little addicted to falling. I would do it for anyone who asked, and sometimes for anyone who didn't. I fell for Mrs. Slotnick, our next-door neighbor, and I fell for the Chaffin girls across the street, crashing onto the floor and standing seconds later, unharmed. Wow. "Wow" was what everyone said.

I went back to school and during recess I fell for the kids. "Look at this," I said, and I dive-bombed down in a cloud of playground dust, and after that a few of the boys wanted lessons from me, which I gladly gave, for a small fee.

Was I happy? This, this is the happy part of my story, which does not mean I was happy. I felt proud, though, and I long ago learned what everyone should know, that dignity counts more than delight.

At night, sometimes, I heard her moving in the kitchen beneath my bedroom, and I crept down the stairs to watch her. Since I'd come back, she had changed as well. She had gotten weaker. Or maybe she had always been this weak, but I saw it more. She started smoking Kent cigarettes and drinking red wine, and she had less of an interest in me. She said I would never be a skating star. Sometimes she stared into the space in front of her, and other times she tapped her finger very fast on her chin, over and over, *tap tap tap,* and still other times she went for a whole day without saying a word. I watched her at night. My mother, in her Christian Dior nightgown. She could never sleep. Her whole life she had fought to stay on the surface of things—to not argue with my father in public, to cover her emotions with a flashy smile—and it showed in her face, where lines of deep fatigue were grooved beneath her makeup.

"*Mom Mom,*" I whispered. I always wanted to cry for her. I always will.

But this, this is a happy part of the story, a crash course in learning to live apart. A few weeks after my return from Saint Christopher's, a tragedy happened. Our neighbor Mr. Slotnick had a heart attack while cleaning his pool, and he fell into his pool and died, not from the heart attack, but because he drowned. I hardly knew him, but it was still a tragedy. I went to the funeral with my parents, my first one. I let her do with me what she wanted, a black velvet dress, black tights with diamonds in them, somber pieces of pearl in my ears. I still loved my mother, understand that, please. But something had changed in me, and therefore between us, I could not have said exactly what it was. I didn't want to cry only for her, but *for us,* and sometimes, in the middle of changing a lightbulb or fixing a sink or doing my English homework, I would have the urge to sprint into her lap, bury my face in her bosom, or better yet, do a perfect skating pirouette for her, all the while saying, *You are the one mom one mom one mom there is no one else but you.*

However, that wasn't true. I was having an affair, you see, and it was with the world.

I thought, back then, that the affair would last forever, but now I see why it didn't. Now I see there is a kind of confidence many ten-year-olds have—the age of industry, Erik Erikson said. The age before the breasts have come, and all the small smells that shame you—what a time it is. What a life.

We went to Mr. Slotnick's funeral, along with the rest of the world. It was a very subdued and slightly disappointing affair, especially because in Jewish funerals they keep the coffin closed, so I never even got to see. There was a service, and then we all went to the graveyard, and along the way, the hearse had engine trouble.

Which meant we all arrived at the graveyard first, and for a damn long time stood out in the March wind, looking into a deep crater, already ringed with lilies.

I got bored. Above me gray clouds raced across the sky. I tapped the toe of my party shoe right at the rim of the grave hole.

"Stop that, Lauren," my mother said.

But I couldn't stop. I kept tapping and tapping, and it wasn't because I was having a seizure. "Stop that now!" she hissed, but I didn't want to. In my mind, or maybe it was in the sky, I heard a cardinal singing, "One tap more, oh, one tap more," and there was a whole crowd of people, and I have always been a bit of a show-off, and I was her daughter, yes, but I was more than that too, and so I did it. I buckled my knees, let my limbs loose in the way I had learned, and I collapsed down into the deep hole, the empty grave, where the coffin had yet to be lowered.

I fell for centuries, and as I went down, I opened my mouth, and the cardinal flew out, and was free.

"Oh, my God!" I heard people screaming. I opened my eyes at the bottom of the grave. I searched the crowd for my mother's face. I could not find it, though, in the blur of heads and hands bending down to help me.

So many people have helped me on my way, I want to thank them here. Thanks to the nuns, my physical therapists, especially Rosie and Jane, I couldn't have done it without you; thanks to my father for his wise rabbinical story, and to Dr. Patterson for his diagnostic skills; thanks especially to Leonard Kriegel, essayist par excellence, whose story *Falling into Life,* from which I have so generously borrowed, helped me to find my own true tale; thanks to my good friend Elizabeth, who is critiquing me as I write this book, and to the librarians at Brandeis, who have provided me with so much material, to Lisa Schiffman, Audrey Schulman, Rob Brown, and Meaghan Rady, for listening, and to my editor, Kate Medina, for the contract and the money.

So many hands, so much help, most of it, really, not my mother's.

Thanks to my mother, for having me, for giving me the special kind of grit I later learned to use.

I opened my eyes at the bottom of the grave and there were so many hands extended, I didn't know which one to take. I was unbruised, unharmed, and I knew how to help

myself. So I stood, and brushed the dirt off, and made myself toeholds in the dank earth.

And I climbed up, and up, and, forgive me my imagery,
but I emerged, headfirst, and then bellied my way over the
ledge of the motherland, and as I did, squiggling up, my
torso pressed flat against the walls of wet earth, I felt a
strange, tender pain in my chest, what I didn't know then—
the beginning of breasts.

The End

Not quite.

This is a work of nonfiction. Everything in it is supposed to be true. In some instances names of people and places have been changed to protect their privacy, but the essential story should at least aim for accuracy, so the establishment says. Therefore, I confess. To the establishment. I didn't really fall into the grave. I was just using a metaphor to try to explain my mental state. The *real* truth is I went to the funeral, the hearse had engine trouble, the coffin was late, I looked into the grave, and I thought about falling in. I imagined myself falling in. I knew I could do it. It was eight feet under but, dammit, I knew I could do it. Didn't divers leap from cliffs forty feet into the air? Didn't they enter the crystal water without so much as a smack? Doesn't the body bend and ripple in all sorts of ways we would never believe it could? I closed my eyes. And in my mind I let myself low. And a cardinal came out of my mouth. And when I hit, the soil was soft, and all the sisters came back to greet me, and offered me holy hands, and when I stood, I saw I was back in Kansas, my land of lemon drops and witches, only it was not a dream. I missed my mother, but there are many places other than home, a shame, a blessing both. The nuns were there. And the red doors opened, and I saw I was strong. And all the snow was singing.

CHAPTER 4

SINCERELY, YOURS

JANUARY 18, 1998

DEAR READER:

Every night before dinner I say grace. I light two white tapers, and even though I was born a Jew, I clasp my hands and give thanks to a Christian God for the kindness he has shown.

For most of my life I've had a relationship with God. When I was ten, and learning how to fall, I felt personally connected to God, who also knew how to fall, fleshing out his body and bowing into vulnerable human form. Children understand intuitively that God lives in leaves and skin. I knew God when I was ten, when the nuns touched me and an easy sureness filled my lungs, so even the snow was singing.

I came home from that convent school as strong as

I had ever been. I have a few pictures of me from that time, and, although it was winter, I look mysteriously tan, my body a rich brewed color, my teeth flashing. In those pictures I grin like an imp. I grin like a girl with know-how.

If you had asked me back then, one month, two months after the convent, I would have told you what the mind learns it cannot forget, that the new and bendable body signals the same for the brain. I had no idea how the body changes as it ages, how at ten there is a certain stability to the skin that hormones, and longing, eventually leach away, until you forget the self you once were. I forgot. I grinned like an imp and then I didn't. I turned eleven; I turned twelve; I turned thirteen, and the rich brewed color faded back to the frailer peach of a girl on the edge of sex and weakness.

For me, the adolescent years were not about ripenings. Instead, I felt used up and dependent. If others did not admire me, I thought I would disappear.

I had seizures once a day, sometimes in school. The seizures horrified me; they were thrashing humiliations, especially when I wet my pants. I'm sure it was for this reason alone I did not attain popularity. When I thought of the word *popular* I saw a pert pink flower open in the sun. The sky was blue. A girl smelled good. Not me.

My mother, it turns out, had her own popularity issues. Once, she had thought I might do it for her, be a skating star or a genius. Now, however, I was just a person with a disease. Our paths went wider and wider apart, until at last, one day, I saw I was alone in the woods, with the worms and crows.

And where was she? She turned into a writer of maxims. She said she had an editor by the name of Suki Israel who would one day publish her work. "Dress for the position you want," she wrote, "not the one you have," and "If it's not a beautiful morning, let your cheerfulness make it one."

The year was 1976, and all over the country love was flowering. My mother caught on. Those were the days when you could go into a bookstore and the entire front display would be of happy meditations. On the fridge, where once had hung a picture of me in my red-and-white skating skirt, was now the maxim she said was her best yet: "Even when you don't feel brave, pretend you are, for this is how courage comes."

And so as I went down, down into adolescent sickness and skin, down into daily seizures, she went up, up into the clear air of adage. She sent her work off to Hallmark, to poetry contests listed in the back of *Good Housekeeping*, contests where you had to pay thirty dollars and renew your subscription for the next five years, contests that would turn you into a star. I loved those entry forms, their tiny lines and boxes making it seem so neat, and the promises written in bold black: $8,000 AND A WORLDWIDE READERSHIP! With her pen, she scratched her way toward it.

Sometimes weeks and weeks, months and months, would go by, and she'd get no reply to her submissions. The longer she waited, the happier she got. Oh, she was lovely in her state of limbo, when the whole world stretched out before her, the moon a bright surprise above. "It means," I heard her say on the phone to Nance, or maybe Emma, or maybe

even Suki, "it means I am under serious consideration." I
was not, anymore, under her consideration, serious or otherwise. I was free, free to fall, to smoke, to spit, to kiss; free to
dress in black, or in crushed velvet, or in ratty tuxedo tails, it
was dizzying.

Over and over again, my mother and I crashed, and in
some essential way, we were graceless. Eventually, she
would get a reply, a rejection of course, after which she
would lie in a darkened room for hours. When she cried, it
was for things so utterly separate from me that her tears were
personal insults. I told myself I didn't care. But sometimes I
think all the corruption that followed had to do with the fact
that there was a space between us, and, when I was thirteen,
in an extra rickety world, I needed to fill that space with
something, and it would not be her. I told myself I didn't
care, but my dreams were full of women; women lifting me,
women treading toward me, while above the moon burned
in a beautiful way.

. . .

The spring of my thirteenth year was unlike any other. Frail
rain fell, casting a silver net over the neighborhood. Then
the sky cleared. The sun went down in a pool of red, and all
the flowers smelled like lotion.

A little boy came to our school, a Japanese boy by the
name of Sumio Yakima. I was cruel to him; I told him "thank
you" was pronounced "fuck you," which won me points
with the popular people.

I was inspired. At that point, I was still trying to outrun

my seizures, and I thought I might accomplish that by being mean. I did other cruel things involving lima beans and bananas, the specifics of which I will not mention here. The worst I ever did, though, had nothing to do with hurting another human being. It had to do with God, in whom I believed even back then, and whose name I had promised myself never to take in vain. One day Sarah Kushner gave me a red Magic Marker and dared me to write on the wall "God = shit," which I did for her attentions, and I pinpoint that as the moment when what I meant versus what I said parted ways, and, with a whimper, my adolescence was born.

. . .

Words came in a rush, then, and none of them were mine. "I would love a cerise-colored outfit," I said to Amy Goldblatt on the trolley one day. "I look like an absolute hag," I became fond of announcing in the girls' room during recess, a place with mildewy-smelling green stalls, gunk in the grout of the cracked tile floor, white washbasins with rings of rust around the drains. In there, girls leaned toward the mirrors, fell into their faces' reflections like it was love, like it was hate, snapping open clam-shaped compact cases and patching up their oily skin. Everyone's skin was so oily, and girls squealed like they were only half person and the other half was pig, it was so sad, and I trotted along on my little high hooves with the rest of them, rooting about for beauty.

But no matter how much makeup I wore, I was still a girl with epilepsy, a girl who pissed herself, a girl convulsed; was there a way to make sickness sexy? That was the year I read nineteenth-century novels, in which tubercular heroines coughed up blood, and died in feather beds. I bought foundation two shades lighter than my actual skin. I wore a dark velvet ribbon like a choker around my neck, and I took my Medic Alert bracelet off my wrist and sported it instead as an anklet, the scarlet serpent dangling down.

And still, Sarah Kushner did not invite me to her party Friday night. Danny Harris wouldn't like me. "I am dying," I whispered to Sarah in English class one day.

"You're dying?" she said to me. "What's wrong?"

"Cancer," I said.

"I thought you had epilepsy," she said.

"Epilepsy causes cancer," I said. "Can you believe it?"

She believed it. She invited me to her party lickety-split, and Haskell Crocker danced with me, and Danny Harris held my hand, and every girl brought me pink punch, such beautiful punch, with foamy globs floating on top, and slices of orange and lemon in it. Sweet. Sweet. The whole time, it seemed, Elton John was singing about the sun going down, and I saw it, all the wolves howling while the sun went down, casting steep shadows, marks of sin on me.

. . .

My mother picked me up from that party. Before I left, Sarah said, "You could come again next time." On the one hand, I was thrilled. The cancer story had been a brilliant idea, brilliant. On the other hand, there was something wrong with the tone of her invite. She'd said it in such a soft, gentle way, in a voice so full of pity I felt pathetic.

I got in the car with my mother. I had a numb feeling, and when I looked at my hand it was not mine. That's all I can say.

"Mom?" I asked.

She didn't turn to me, though. She kept driving. Her mouth was grim and pressed while above her passing streetlights floated in her beehive hair. The car so quiet. I saw a dead dog on the side of the road.

I thought I might have a seizure. Sometimes I said a little prayer, "Please, God, prevent it from happening, one, two, three, four, five, six, seven, eight, nine, ten." The counting to ten was the most important part of the prayer.

I prayed then, counted to ten, and looked out. The car hummed along in a smoothly sinister way. I recognized nothing, not the houses, not the yards. "Where are we?" I said.

Still, she didn't answer.

"Mom!" I yelled.

Then she answered. Her voice clacked out of her throat like a prerecorded message. "Calm down," she said.

"Where are we going?" I said. "This isn't the way home."

"I am running an errand," she said.

I rolled down my window and air, clean and fresh, rushed in, filled my mouth like sweet lake water when you dive down. Through the dense night, I saw we had entered a new kind of neighborhood, a place where the houses were sprawling and pillared, where blue pools lapped and the lawns were wide.

My mother pulled over and turned off the car. "Wait here," she said. Ahead of us stood a massive home.

"What errand are you running?" I said.

"My editor, Suki Israel," she said. "I just need to drop off some work. I'll be right back."

And then she wafted up the white brick walk, a door mysteriously opened, she sucked into the dazzle of light. And then gone.

I waited.

At first only five minutes passed, then what seemed like ten, and then I lost track of time. It was April, and the night grew chilly, and frost fell on the windshield. I wanted to cry.

I waited some more. The car engine, still hot, ticked, and stopped. I thought it was possible my mother wasn't coming back. I stepped out of the car, then, and heard a stillness that was not of this world. It was the stillness of a stage set, of a madman's sleeping mind. I crept toward a window.

What I saw inside there I will not forget. Huge aquariums were built into every wall, jellyfish like lamps in the green water, octopi bobbing, my mother nowhere around. It was beautiful in a frightening way. I saw, then, how essentially ahuman the world was, a place where the real turned to waves, and washed away.

I went back to the car. What felt like a long time later she emerged, smoothing her skirt, her hair slightly mussed—or did I just imagine that?—smiling now as she stepped down the path, and when I said, "It's been hours, Mom," she said, "It's been minutes, Lauren," and I got so confused—water, vapor, twisted time—that right then I felt a craving in me, a craving for something safe and solid and absolutely absolute.

. . .

That was the night I started to steal. Maybe I'm wrong. Maybe I really started to steal a few days after that, or a few weeks before. Maybe it's just certain narrative demands, a need for neatness compelling me to say *that was the night* or *and this led surely to this,* my life a long link of daisies, a bolt of cloth unbroken, I wish it were.

So, that night. If not that night, I assure you it was around then.

I stepped onto our lawn. Around me, I could see the more modest homes of our neighborhood, and they comforted me in their familiar size and shape. Across the street from us, the Slotnicks grew cherry tomatoes in the summer, and Mrs. Slotnick always brought me some, vitamin C, she said, being the cure for every disease.

Now, I walked toward the Slotnicks' house. I remembered how, years ago, when I was ten, I had rung people's bells and waited in the bushes, loving it when, for just one moment, a door opened toward me, a place of possible comfort.

I thought I would do that again, ring a buzzer and hide, nothing more. But, instead, when I got to the Slotnicks' front door, I turned the handle and slipped in.

Houses hold us, and all that is dear in our worlds. I slipped in, and felt the walls curve to cup me, and smelled roasted chicken and other just general living odors, sweat and steel wool pads leaving swaths of blue soap that are beautiful. A home has many purposes, but it should primarily be a place where you can cry and run a good fever.

And as I stood there, hunched in the Slotnicks' front hall, I had a sense of immense peace, and then longing. This is how it started. I looked around me. I heard someone moving in the next room. I didn't want to be caught. On the hall table was a hat. There was an umbrella with a few broken ribs and on the wall, surrounded by other photos, a picture in a plain wood frame, an old-fashioned photograph of a lady in a garden, her hands heaped with greens. "My Aunt Henrietta," Mrs. Slotnick had once told me.

I looked at Aunt Henrietta, happy in her garden, her whole body sepia-soft, and I thought how good it would be to have her. So I took her. It wasn't a big deal, it was just one picture, and a little one at that, so I took her. I slipped her in my pocket, and before I left the house I saw the small space I had made on the Slotnicks' wall, a gap in the middle of human history where Henrietta used to be, and for a minute I felt full, the emptiness now outside of me.

. . .

Things become addictions for no good reason except that you started them. If that night I had gone to my parents' liquor cabinet and poured myself a shot of Scotch, then it probably would have been Scotch that sang to me forever after.

However, it wasn't Scotch. I became addicted to tchotchkes, anything solid and small enough to fit in the palm of my hand, people's personal possessions with their personal smells still on them. What I liked even more was the thievery itself, the rush and spice of it, how for one moment I could step into a place so steeped in adrenaline the world was real and rimmed with red. I didn't know then that the word *epilepsy* comes from the Greek word *epilepsia*, which means "to take, to seize." My body had become epileptic years ago, but when I turned thirteen, so did my soul.

What I stole: a small tin filled with pennies from the Shocketts' house; an egg timer, also from the Shocketts' house; a mug with Bugs Bunny on it; an anchor-shaped paperweight. I never once stole from a store. (All right, once.) I stole from the houses in the neighborhood where I lived, edging my way in, the carpets sucking up the sound of my footsteps, the family, unsuspecting, eating meat loaf in the kitchen. I stashed all my goods in the toolshed out back, the one my father never used ("He can't even figure out how to hold a hammer," my mother would sometimes say, scornfully). The toolshed was itself like a little house, brown flower boxes beneath its windows. It was a world, and as it filled with my goods, it became my world. Sometimes I would go out there at night, just as the springtime sun was setting with a soft hiss, and the light was full of richness. The blue mug glowed; the tins quietly twinkled. I felt a satisfaction come over me then, and I would sit on the buckled brown floor of the shed, and hug my knees, and watch.

...

I got my period. This was a disappointment. In school we had a book on teenage emotions, in which there was a whole chapter devoted to the emotions around getting your period. The book said you would feel full of things, water and grief and little sparkles of joy.

When my period came, you could barely even tell. I had imagined blood spooling generously from inside. Instead, there was just a brownish little flow, like rusty trickles from an old tap. I kept waiting for an emotion or two, but all I could feel was worried that I didn't have an emotion, or two.

What happened was this. Soon after menstruation, the seizures worsened, which is sometimes the case with females, hormones egging on the brain, estrogen tweaking the system. My nipples pegged out and my seizures came fast now, came furious, one a day no, two a day no, three, four, five a day, each one with a full-blown aura. I want to talk about the auras. I lost my social life, I lost my body, I lost my mother, I lost this, I lost that, everyone could see me but me when I went down, and so I don't want to talk about the seizures. I want to talk about the auras, which many epileptics have and agree are truly special states. My auras. They were with me almost constantly after my period, states of light and sizzle, states of joy and trees, states of dread laced through with terrific sweet smells, the tongue so very alive.

Seizures are not just spasms. That's called a grand mal, or tonoclonic, and it was my most common type, but I had other types too. Some seizures are very subtle, just a twitch of the eye, and others are funny, a person, maybe, repeating a phrase over and over, or walking backward for no good reason. In school I started to say, "Wait. Wait just a minute!" I didn't always fall on the floor. Once, so they tell me, I got up in the middle of math class and tried to climb out the window. I don't remember that. I just remember smelling orange marmalade.

This I do remember. Since the epilepsy had begun three years ago, functioning was always difficult, but now it was almost impossible. I just gave up. People, always wary of me, now made wide, careful arcs around me in the hall, and once, in the lunchroom, when I asked Amy Goldblatt for a sip of her Coke, she paused and then said, "Oh, sure, have the whole can," and I knew it was because she didn't want to put her mouth where mine had been. I didn't go to Sarah Kushner's parties, and I didn't dance with boys, and I knew not even the cancer story would change these facts.

I saw that success, if I were to have it, would be not outside, but within, my sickness. Sometimes I went down for hours, and when I woke up a whole day had passed, me dreaming through time on the spikes and jags of seizures. If it happened in school, I might wake up in the sickroom, a place, like the toolshed, that I came to crave. There was a nurse named Nell Fiore with baby-doll blue eyes. "Fiore," she would say, "pronounced like *fjord,*" a word I knew, and I pictured it, a place of clean green water, the air delicious.

"You've had a bad one," Nell might say. "Shall we send you home?"

"No."

I lay on the narrow metal cot. She put her hands on my forehead, and if I'd bitten my mouth she cleaned it with something that fizzed and tasted of lime. Sometimes I watched TV in the school's sickroom, a movie, I remember, about World War II, and it all seemed oddly beautiful, bombs drifting down through the evening air like sinister silver angels, the perpetual fall of German snow. There was a world out there, but I didn't have to be part of it, and slowly I saw the privilege of this. It must have been in the sickroom where illness became not a thing I had but a thing through which I could escape. It was a secret door in the back of a Victorian closet, and when I went through it I entered something soundless and secluded, a place of pure float. Through the thin walls I might hear the other world, the difficult world where maybe women were cold, where there was chalk trotting across a blackboard, Latin verbs declined down to their raw nubs, the titter of growing girls; I was free from that. I was safe. I saw hot-air balloons and lovely ladies fed me salted limes, and in this place, my place, I stayed small forever.

. . .

His name was Dr. Neu, pronounced like *oy,* and he looked like a Yiddisher too, a little frumpy and old-fashioned, with thick eyebrows and a curly beard. As soon as I saw him I wanted to touch his beard, because it was curly, but also because it was red, like a living fox, tipped here and there with white.

He was my new doctor at Beth Israel, my brilliant neurologist who had published many articles, one of which I will include later in this book. Everyone, epileptic or not, should read the work of Dr. Neu, because he understands the philosophy of neurology, how the cellular phenomenon called consciousness is so much more than a blip of energy; it's a blue light, a flame we can feel but cannot find; it's mystery and love.

I loved Dr. Neu, almost right away. I went to see him because my case got so severe, and also because I wasn't a child anymore. So I said good-bye to my pediatrician, Dr. Patterson, and hello to Dr. Neu. I went up to the sixth floor at Beth Israel and waited in his waiting room. He called me in and looked me over. He said, "So, I hear you are quite a case," and then he smiled.

I smiled back. "I suppose I am," I said, trying to sound weary and elegant.

"Sit," he said, patting the table.

I considered hopping up on the table, but that seemed very unladylike. I smoothed my skirt. I was afraid if I jumped up, he might see my underwear. I smoothed my skirt again and then he said, "Oh, may I offer you some assistance?" and he brought over a stool, and he held my hand as I stepped up on it, like I was a queen coming into a carriage.

"Thank you so much," I said. The sound of my voice, even though it was not my own, pleased me. It was crisp and a bit British. Dr. Neu smiled.

"My pleasure," he said.

. . .

Like I said, he was not a normal neurologist. He was a brilliant man, and brilliance is never normal. His office was all stainless steel, white drapery, the sheen of surgical tools. In one corner he had a plaster human head with removable parts. I held in my hands the thalamus, the cerebellum, the substantia nigra. "Intelligence," Dr. Neu said, "is not the sum of its parts. It's even more."

I didn't know what he meant, but it moved me. I could almost cry listening to him. What did I need with anyone else? I had him, and Nell Fiore, the sickroom and my sickness, and as time went by it all started to seem like enough.

Dr. Neu, of course, had a different agenda. His mission was to cure me, and in order to do that he needed to find out where in my brain the seizures started. He called my parents and me in for a conference. "We need to know where," he said. "And in order to find the locale, we will do some exploratory surgery."

"Why do you need to know where?" my mother said. "Does where matter? It's not a question of where," she said. "It's a question of is. We know the epilepsy is. You don't have to cut open her head to prove that."

"At this point," said Dr. Neu, "I am not talking about cutting open her whole head. Only a small piece. It's a harmless procedure."

"Will she have a visible scar?" my mother asked.

"Beneath the hairline," Dr. Neu said, and that disappointed me a little. Of course I wanted something shiny and pink and tremendously obvious, like a love tattoo.

He did the exploratory surgery on a Wednesday. He recommended that I rest for the few days before, so I got to miss school on Monday and Tuesday, great. I lay in my shade-darkened room, my mother running errands, my father at work, the house so quiet I could hear the ticking of branches, the gurgle of the fridge. I sat in front of the mirror and combed my hair. I had never noticed before what beautiful hair I had. It was a chestnut brown; it bounced and glistened. It was the precise color of my eyes, I matched.

. . .

And then Wednesday. I was dressed in a white johnny, with blue scrub slippers over my bare feet. The OR was frosty, the steel table cool beneath my body. Dr. Neu and two other doctors came in. Dr. Neu said, "It's such a simple procedure, Lauren. We're not even going to put you to sleep. We're just going to give you some Novocain in your scalp, so it won't hurt when we cut."

I was not afraid. They had described to me how the doctors would make a small slit in my scalp, and then touch the surface of my brain with an electrical stimulator. It would not hurt; it would not take long, but I might feel a few funny things every once in a while.

"Okay," Dr. Neu said, standing above me. I felt him sawing at my skull, Jesus, and then the suck of something lifted, like the lid from an airtight cookie jar. "We're close now. Soon you might feel something funny."

He had the electrical stimulator in his hand. I saw it. It looked like this:

And then I held my breath. I felt myself go very still, the fear. Now, now I was afraid. They had promised me it would not hurt; they had told me the brain, which is the seat of all feeling, has no nerves in it. How could that be? The brain seemed to me to be as tender as the tongue, each bump a bud with which to taste the world. I heard a small zap. "Okay," Dr. Neu said. And all my fear went away. I saw yellow, puffs and puffs of it, a yellow so pure, so true, it seemed extracted from the center of the sun.

"I see colors," I said.

"Yes," said Dr. Neu. "That's because we're stimulating your visual cortex."

I watched the yellow. After a while it moved into my mouth, and I tasted lemons and soil. I smacked my tongue. "Are you having taste sensations?" Dr. Neu asked.

"Yes," I said. The word *yes* had a taste too; it was like speaking through a strawberry sucker.

"Pleasurable tastes, I hope," Dr. Neu said.

"Yes," I said.

"And now?" he said.

"Voices," I said. "I hear voices. I hear a woman calling me," and she was calling me, this woman, standing by a brick house in a long forgotten place. "Lauren, Lauren, Lauren," and when I turned I saw her with her hands cupped round her cry and all the grass was moving.

"And now?" Dr. Neu said. I had caught on to what he was doing. He was moving the probe from place to place on my bare brain, and each time he moved it, a new color, a new taste, probing all the pieces of me back so fast it was salmon swimming upstream, a surge beneath glassy water, and then there was that woman again—who was she?—walking down a flagstone path, and it filled me with a feeling like I wanted to cry; I did cry. "She's crying," I heard someone say, and I heard Dr. Neu say, "If only Freud could witness this, the material id." And that was when it happened. The material id, he said, and right after that a pure sensation went through me, a sensation that flickered up and down the length of my spine like a spark travels the tail of dynamite, getting closer, getting closer, it was good, it was touch, it was true: "You're tickling my back," I said to Dr. Neu, and even when he said, "No, I'm not, I'm in the somatosensory cortex," I didn't believe him. I believed he was touching me, and that he might learn to love me after a while.

He was not touching me, he never was, but that was the year when what was and what could be—the real and the reflected, the true and the false—got all mixed up and merged together. I believed he was touching me; keep this in mind as events unfold. I believed he was. I had four more electrical probes after that one, and each time I would stay over in the hospital while my head healed up. Sometimes, also, I would stay over in the hospital for CAT scans, for angiograms, for extended encephalograms. I loved the beds that rose up and dipped down. I loved ordering my food from a menu and getting my meals in little packets, a present, each part. I loved socializing with the nurses, who liked me and played Parcheesi with me as late as 10:00 P.M. I was practically popular on the ward. In addition, the sheets were softer than at home, and people touched you kindly, and low lights burned all through the night.

What happened is this. The rest of the world began to feel far away, a land I no longer knew how to live in. I felt bad for everyone in this land, and I looked at them with scorn.

Instead of learning to live in the land, I went to the doctor's almost every day after school, and once or twice a week I slept over at the hospital, packing my red carrying case like I was going to a girlfriend's house. I looked forward to socializing with the nurses in the solarium. When I wasn't there, I missed them and thought about when I'd go back. I started to have a daydream in which it was always winter. Dressed in a Lycra skirt, bright white skates laced around my petite legs, I looked as perfect as a toy. In my daydream I skimmed over the ice, cold shavings flying from my blades while people stood in the bleachers and clapped. This was the Olympics, and I was winning the world. People clapped as I jumped into the air, came down on a rose tossed into the rink. My balance buckled. I was not at fault. I fell like a winner, like a warrior; I fell with all the innocence of a victim. When I woke up, I was in a hospital and a doctor who spoke French was healing me with his hands. With his hands he worked my broken bones like they were Lincoln Logs, snapping me softly into place. He fixed everything except my left leg, which instead he plastered in a cast. I went back into the world like that, and everyone who saw me said, "Oh. Oh. I'm sorry."

Sometimes, if I had this daydream in bed, I would fall asleep before it was finished. Other times I would get to the end only to start the story all over again, only this time I had broken not only my bones, but many of my organs too, and the doctor who spoke French had to work on me using many experimental cures.

Understand, I would have told no one back then. The experimental cures involved pins and touch. Maybe I was becoming mentally ill. Actually, I was becoming mentally ill. If you've read my other books—and I have written other books, *Prozac Diary* and *Welcome to My Country,* which I suggest you rush out and buy—you would know that mental problems have been issues throughout my life.

Is epilepsy mental or is it physical? A long time ago, when van Gogh was alive, people with epilepsy were put in insane asylums, where I'm sure, with their froth, they fit right in. In my own life, even though she pooh-poohed psychoanalysis, Dr. Swan had once told me my seizures were the result of repressed things, and if I could just let my feelings fly free I would get better. I had asked Dr. Neu about that and he said bosh, and he's brilliant, whereas Dr. Swan was merely bright. But still. When I look back on myself now, from the vantage point of many years, and see myself as I was, all thrash and spasm, I have to wonder what it meant, if my sickness was like longing for things in the past I had never had, and for things in the future I was too afraid to try.

...

"We might be able to cure you pretty soon," Dr. Neu said to me one day.

"What?" I said.

"Cure you," he said. "I think you have the type of seizure that would respond well to a sectioning of your corpus callosum."

I knew the corpus callosum from the model in his office, a creek that cuts through the middle of the brain, where thick bands of fibers connect the separate sides.

The operation didn't scare me, but the hospital, that I might lose the hospital. "I've been feeling," I said, "significantly worse, you know."

My voice had a thick sound, as though coming up through clots in my throat. *Don't cry,* I thought. *Whatever you do, don't cry.*

"Oh," he said, sitting down in a chair, "how is that?"

Lately, in my spare time, I'd been going to the library and reading about my disease, and now I started to pull out phrases I could recall. While I spoke I watched my doctor's face, the living red beard, the wide, kind hands. *Don't leave me,* I was thinking.

Don't cry, I was thinking, because, you see, I did not want to give myself away.

"The seizures," I said, stretching my memory, "the, the neural discharge, it's been far faster. More rapid," I said, because that was what I had read in a book.

"Rapid," he said. "More rapid?" A small smile formed on

his face, but I was so desperate it didn't occur to me he could see right through me; I took the smile as a sign of interest.

"Yes," I said. "I have terrible headaches. Terrible! Terrible! There may be a tumor too."

"Where?" he said, leaning forward. "Where, Lauren, do you think this tumor is?"

"I feel it here," I said, touching the crown of my head, the place where long ago the plates of bone should have grown together, but, on me, a soft spot still.

. . .

I went home on the trolley, holding hard to a steel pole while the car clattered over tracks. At every station-stop I stared out the grime-speckled windows and saw the world through a scrim of speckled grime; ugly. At last we left the city behind and climbed up out of the underground, into the air of green neighborhoods, where children swung a rope and sang:

> *Old Mr. Kelly had a pimple on his belly*
> *His wife bit it off and it tasted like jelly*

So this was the world out there, no thank you. And yet, my seizures were exhausting, and when I saw certain boys, truth be told, I did get a funny feeling in my mouth and in my innards, like maybe there was something to want out there, in the frightening but occasionally pretty place where girls swirled with color and people held hands.

. . .

I got off at my stop—Waban—and started home, the same way every day, past the baseball diamond and then the Newton-Wellesley, a small suburban hospital. On this day, though, I didn't pass the Newton-Wellesley. Instead I turned right and went into the emergency room.

In my hands, that feeling, like I wanted to steal. The pneumatic doors parted. In front of me a woman slouched in a plastic chair. In the far corner I saw another woman, altogether happier looking, a baby snoozing in a car seat by her side. Oh, that baby was cute. Even from the distance I could tell.

I went closer, close enough so I could see the small sunsets in each of his pale fingernails, and the little dark dots of his nostrils.

The mother smiled at me.

"Mrs. Carney?" a nurse said, and Mrs. Carney got up, looking back once at the baby while she crossed the room to the reception booth.

What I had: a desire to feel the flesh of the baby, so plentiful I could smell its talc. I liked the baby's mouth, the red spurt of its smile, and its booties, with just the tiniest bells sewn in. The baby kicked, and the bells went off. Such a merry thing. I wanted the baby, or at least its booties, and I saw how simple it would be to steal it.

I could just pick up the baby and go. Apparently, all you had to do to steal a baby was to pick it up and go. If so, then maybe all you had to do to become a baby was, was to pick it up and go? To steal a baby? To steal its booties? Understand,

I am mentally ill. I didn't want the baby, but to be the baby. I crept closer still, and then, just as I was getting up my very troubled guts to do something with either the baby or the booties, the mother came back, saying, "Okay then, Miranda, we'll see you next week," and she swooped up the child and left through the circling glass door.

I got mad. I have a lot wrong with me, psychologically speaking, but I have always been a sweet-tempered person. After the woman left, though, I felt rage inside of me, and I thought, *Fuck fuck fuck.*

I gripped my hands hard. *Let me have a seizure,* I thought. I started it myself. I'd never brought on a seizure before, and I hadn't known it was possible. I swayed back and forth and squinched up my eyes and I thought of rubbing rocks together until a small spark catches, and crackles, I went. One. Two. Three. I caught. I sank myself down and started it myself, arsonist of the flesh. Wind rocked through me and pollution poured out my ears, and when I awoke, what do you think?

Doctor of my dreams, he was standing over me, with another doctor, and several nurses, and a private curtain making the cubicle my own.

"What happened?" I said, even though I knew.

The nurse drew blood. She nosed a needle under my skin and I watched the tube fill. My blood seemed especially red that day, like it was ashamed and excited, both.

Someone called my mother, who came to pick me up, and in all the hubbub no one thought to ask me why I was in the

ER in the first place. What I was doing was no different than stealing, really. Instead of taking things, I was taking time; taking attention—

Taking touch.

. . .

And so it happened. Our heroine began her criminal career lifting small concrete tchotchkes from small suburban houses, and she ended it in the abstract, stealing things beyond weight, beyond measure. I was a very Piagetian thief. After the first ER, I made my visits regular. I lived in Boston, where there are almost as many hospitals as there are people to fill them. The Deaconess, the Children's, the Peter Bent Brigham and the Lying-In. The Mary Saltonstall, Mount Auburn and Mass General, the Lindemann and the Dana. After school, I would drop in to different ERs, and stage a seizure, and wake up in that wonderful way, wake up in a blizzard of nurses, a cup of cool water held to my lips, oh.

Oh.

"I'm okay," I would say, struggling like a heroine to sit up.

"No no. Stay still. Lie down. Rest."

The Saltonstall, the Peter Bent Brigham, the Lying-In, all wonderful, rhythmic names, all old brick buildings with twinkling views of the city.

"I can get up," I would say again. I had, after all, gotten what I'd needed, and now I knew I could leave.

"Where do you live? We'll call your parents," the nurses would say.

I'd figured this one out. Certainly I couldn't have my mother called each time; she would have caught on. Instead, I gave the nurses the number of a pay phone by my town's trolley stop. The decrepit-looking pay phone hunched by itself in a corner, a phone no one would answer when it rang. It must have rung and rung in the nurses' ears. I pictured the phone ringing in the late-day dark of June, and sometimes, despite myself, I would hope a person might answer—hello?—and I would have to say, "Yes. Hello. My name is—"

Lauren. Lauren.

I live at—

But I didn't live as Lauren. I lived, in those emergency rooms, as April, Bobby, Maria and Juliette.

"I am epileptic," Juliette said. She showed the nurses her epilepsy bracelet. "I have seizures all the time. I'm fine. Really. I can go now."

And so they let her go. Sometimes, they gave her money for a cab, other times a trolley token. Whatever she got, she saved in a silver pig.

. . .

Munchausen's is the name. A long time ago there lived a man named Munchausen, a German gentleman who traveled from town to town, faking illness. Mr. Munchausen had a waxed dagger mustache, and his hair, swept off his high forehead, made him look as though he faced a forceful wind.

Even though I have never met Mr. Munchausen, and many differences exist between us, he a man with a mus-

tache, I a woman with pierced ears, I feel I know him. I know
his wandering from place to place, his desire for a doctor always. He was so good at illness, a whole disorder has been
named for him, Munchausen's syndrome, otherwise called
factitious illness, the patient faking not for money but for
things beyond weight, beyond measure.

Now we get to a little hoary truth in this tricky tale. The
summer I was thirteen I developed Munchausen's, on top of
my epilepsy, or—and you must consider this, I ask you
please to consider this—perhaps Munchausen's is all I ever
had. Perhaps I was, and still am, a pretender, a person who
creates illnesses because she needs time, attention, touch, because she knows no other way of telling her life's tale. Munchausen's is a fascinating psychiatric disorder, its sufferers
makers of myths that are still somehow true, the illness a
conduit to convey real pain. So you will understand Munchausen's syndrome better, here are some quotes:

FROM: *The British Journal of Psychiatry*, VOLUME I, PP. 227-35

> We have treated a woman by the name of Sheila, a 34
> year old single white female who lived at the time with
> her mother in a rowhouse in Leeds. Sheila had been
> engaged to be married, and she claimed she had loved
> her fiancé "with all my heart." She describes herself as
> subservient to the point of ego extinction, cleaning,
> cooking, trying to anticipate his every wish. When, one
> day, the gentleman announced he was breaking the

engagement, Sheila was devastated. Shortly after that, she announced to her office mates (she worked as a typist in Leeds) that she had breast cancer, and so her performance might not be up to par. Everyone rallied around Sheila, and they even took up a collection for her, but she refused the money. "I can do it on my own," she told them, and her seeming stoicism only made her cohorts admire her more.

Sheila joined a breast cancer support group, shaved her hair so as to look as though she was having chemotherapy, and lost seventeen pounds. She devoted hours and hours to sculpting the life of a cancer patient, and appeared to derive great sustenance from the sympathy offered her by her colleagues. Two years passed, and Sheila sensed that people were beginning to lose interest in her plight. It was at that point that she began to bleed herself on a regular basis, causing her alarmingly white complexion, her chronic fainting fits, and her low cell count.

FROM: *The Journal of Existential Psychiatry,*
VOLUME 112, PP. 9–24

Dr. Ford treated a man with multiple skin lesions refusing to heal. He had over forty hospital admissions for bloody nodules on his thighs and buttocks. One afternoon, a nurse observed this man with a syringe, and a more thorough search of his room revealed several syringes plus cornstarch, with which this patient was willfully injecting himself, so as to cause chronic bacterial infections.

FROM: *The Annals of Psychiatry*, VOLUME 98, PP. 38–44

We have noted that epilepsy is one of the illnesses frequently chosen by Munchausen's patients, and that, despite the stubbornness with which they cling to their illness facades, they also desire to be revealed. They at once deny their perpetual chicanery while, at the same time, leave clues as to the truth. For instance, we have recently treated an adolescent girl whom we shall call Jean Levy. This girl had absolutely no physiological evidence of any epileptic activity. On the one hand, she rather masterfully succeeded in convincing people that she suffered from temporal lobe seizures, to the point where she wrote and published an account of her illness, and yet on the other hand, she prominently placed a book entitled *Patient or Pretender* on the shelf in her hospital room. This child was bright, engaging, and extremely convincing; like most Munchausen's patients, she was an excellent storyteller, well versed in what Adorno so aptly called "the jargon of authenticity." Munchausen's patients have learned to convey authenticity to their audiences precisely by admitting to a limited number of lies. This young girl, for instance, admitted to exaggerating some of her epileptic seizures, but she maintained the baseline veracity of her disorder. In the case of this young patient, and of the many other Munchausen's sufferers, epilepsy seems to be the disease most able to capture and express conflicts with repressed sexuality, poor body image, and deeply impaired sense of self mastery.

Well, that should prove my point. You can fake epilepsy. I admit I sometimes faked my epilepsy, but I also really had it. Still, once I realized I could set off seizures at will, I did it at all the right times and in all the right places. The Peter Bent Brigham. The Lying-In.

Tiring. And how dislike yourself. From my bout with Munchausen's, I now know for a fact we are moral creatures, and that to be anything but is to violate our most basic physiologies. The lying hurt, physically. My head felt on fire, and yet my skin seemed snowy and far away. I started taking baths, long hot soaks, my skin turning tender and red; *here I am.*

I fixed my face up carefully when I went to see Dr. Neu. Back then there was a line of products called Love's Baby Soft. I used all Love's Baby Soft products, rouge in two small circles on my cheeks.

Is it possible that Lauren loved him if there was no Lauren? Was it Juliette who loved him, or Bobby with her floral smells? Who cried in her heart when he touched her head? Dr. Neu was Dutch, and his words had a feathery feel to them. I loved him for no other reason, perhaps, than his voice, how he made every word warm.

My mother, father, and I went in for a meeting with him

one Tuesday at 3:00 P.M. Summer had arrived, and the air was so hot it hung between the trees like breath.

I remember the heat, and I remember the cool clasp of air as soon as we entered the lobby, the switch so sudden it was almost painful.

"Come in," Dr. Neu said. He took us not into his examining room but into his office, where serene music played.

"Sit," he said.

"She needs an operation," he said. "I have thought about it carefully. I have explored the physiology of her seizures and, despite their eliopathic nature, I think a sectioning of the corpus callosum is warranted."

"Oh," we all said.

He went on to explain. He would cut the corpus callosum in my brain, thereby disconnecting the left and right hemispheres, a very common procedure in epileptic children with some, but few, significant side effects. With the brain split, the seizures starting in one side would not spread to the other, and so I should experience a real reduction in illness.

But wait a minute, I wanted to say. *I'm not as ill as I seem.*

"You mean to tell me," my mother said, "that you want to perform a lobotomy on my daughter?"

"It's not a lobotomy," he said. "Surgery is sometimes the method of choice when the pediatric patient does not respond to medication. The procedure will have no effect on her IQ or on her social skills. The side effects are very subtle."

They all had a long conversation then about subtlety and side effects, but I had stopped listening. I noticed my mother looked worn down, and sometime, over the years, grooves of disappointment had deepened by her mouth. She had had such high hopes, she must have entered life with such a lunge, and now, at this midpoint, what? A daughter with a brain disease, a husband in the bakery business, and all the while she with the scent of perfume that trailed her like a scarf. Once she had fought my illness with fists and money, but I had been younger then, and so had she. Once she had watched me seize with something like love in her eyes. But I had been younger then, and so had she. I think, that day in the doctor's office, she just decided to take a rest. I applaud you, Mom, at least the left side of me does, while the right wonders why, why did you let them do it? Why did you let me go? I saw her lie down on the ground. In my mind I imagined her stretching out on Dr. Neu's cream-colored carpet while in real life she nodded, tilted her head, talked to the doctor and my father, and sometime then or a few days later, she said yes to the surgeon; yes to the slice.

Another memory of that time: my father praying. I, waking early in the morning, and seeing my father with the glossy tallis on his shoulders, and a small silver star in his hands.

"So that you might get better," he said. "So you stay safe."

In the weeks before the operation, time speeded up. I wanted to say, "Wait. Wait just a minute. I've made my epilepsy seem worse than it is." I said nothing, half from fear, half from confusion. I had always believed there could be two truths, truth A and truth B, but in my mind truth A sat on top of truth B, or vice versa. In this instance, however, I had epilepsy, truth A, and I had faked epilepsy, truth B, and A and B were placed in a parallel position, instead of one over the other, so I couldn't decide. I had bad dreams at night, dreams in which I found myself skiing fast down a steep slope, and monkeys hung from all the trees.

One day I said to Dr. Neu, "Are you sure I really need this operation?" And he said, "Yes," and that made me feel a little better. He had long talks with me in the hospital cafeteria, telling me I would be his patient for years to come, because even long after the operation he would have to keep studying my brain. I saw my future then. Maybe during the day I would have a career, but I would always come back here, where they would be waiting with thermometers and foot soaks, and if I ever did anything wrong, if I couldn't get into college or forever flunked Mrs. Bezen's math class, no one could blame me, for I was sick and being studied by a surgeon.

Lying on a hospital bed, or on my own bed at home, I had these thoughts. Maybe I would even move into Dr. Neu's house so he could study me twenty-four-seven. We shared a world, that I knew, for the doctor and the patient are bound by necessities more urgent than the love between a husband and a wife, or two best friends; they are bound by the body, and so long as the body lives, so does their love.

And I was pleased with these thoughts, and I was also displeased with these thoughts, with the way I wanted to escape.

I once, years later, met a priest and I said, "What is sin?" and he said, "Sin is the refusal of responsibility," and as soon as he said it I saw he was right, and I apprenticed myself to him.

Six days, five days, four days. A great fear came over me. I was going to have my brain cut. A great darkness came over me, for I knew I was a thief and a liar and it felt wrong on a very basic biological level. I read a story about a tribe of people who live in the mountains in Africa, and sometimes invisible beings called dabs came to steal their souls. A dab, perhaps, had come to steal my soul, because I thought I could recall how once I'd been a different kind of girl, a girl who went in the snow with nuns and said what was on her mind.

And then, the night before the actual operation, while I was lying in my hospital room, I saw the dab who'd stolen my soul. I opened my eyes in the late night, and there was a thing flying and flying around my bed, an angel the size of someone's thumb; I said, "Come here," and the dab said, "No."

When I opened my eyes again, morning had come, and without even opening my window I could see the heat wave had broken; the air looked crisp, the flowers in the beds all bright.

I stood and looked out the hospital window at the cars on the road below, the world awake now, moving in one direction, me moving in another. Where, I wondered, had Lauren gone? Where, I wondered, had my mother gone? And then

I felt what I had not allowed myself to feel, the longing for her love, and the longing for a younger, braver self, a self who had once said a definite yes to living in the world.

Down in the parking lot below me, a station wagon turned in and Dr. Neu stepped out from the passenger's side. The sight of him outside the hospital shocked me. The sight of his wife—his life outside the hospital—shocked me. She stepped out to hug him, a curly-haired woman in a green dress. And then, of course, next came the kid, stepping out to hug him, and this put me over the edge. First, that he had so many people to hug him, his world so wide, I was just a tiny piece, I saw that then. And second, the kid herself. I was twelve stories up but I had, just then, bionic vision. I could see her wheat-colored hair, the bright sneakers on her feet— she was nine, maybe ten—and then I was inside her head, in the world before the body changes, before all the separations start, in a world where you are so surefooted and you believe you can be many things.

I cried then, like I should have cried a long time ago, a coiling cry coming out of me, a nurse rushing to my side, "What's wrong, what's wrong?" I was shaking but it wasn't a seizure, it wasn't a sickness; it was me this time, it was real this time, my sadness and longing coming out and my hands, for once, staying still, not stealing a thing. I did not flee from the feeling but let it puddle up in my throat and go straight out of me, my sound, *the* sound, guttural and wet, salty to the taste, a sound like Lauren, here I am, Lauren living.

It was Lauren, then, who lay on the table in the OR, Lauren who felt the needle of lidocaine slide into her scalp, Lauren who heard the whining of the saw and felt the pressure from his hands and the cutting devices, Lauren who fancied she heard the snapping sound of disconnecting tissue, and the cool air that came to fill the cleft where her connections had once been, and the whole time it happened it was Lauren who hung on to the sound of her cry, a sound without pretense or mask, true-tongued and absolutely absolute—remember this, remember this, no, not you, Juliette, not you, Bobby, not Maria or Kayla or April or June but Lauren—

Love, Lauren

THE BIOPSYCHOSOCIAL CONSEQUENCES OF A CORPUS CALLOSTOMY IN THE PEDIATRIC PATIENT

DR. CARLOS NEU, M.D., AND
PATRICIA ROBINSON, P.T.

ABSTRACT

Sixty percent of patients with temporal lobe epilepsy display dysfunctional psychological profiles that include emotional lability; mythomania, with all its attendant exaggerations and untruths; tendency toward melodrama, hypergraphia and hyper-religiosity. This paper addresses the degree to which a successful surgical intervention that reduces or eliminates tonoclonic seizures can concomitantly reduce or eliminate the epileptic's dysfunctional personality style. This paper also addresses the importance of postsurgery rehabilitation that takes into account the complexity of epilepsy as a biopsychosocial phenomenon.

INTRODUCTION

While we once conceptualized epilepsy as a solely physical illness with few, if any, personality correlates, we now, thanks to the insights of Geschwind (1963) and Bear (1981), view temporal lobe epilepsy in a more complex fashion—as both a seizure *and* a personality disorder. A significant number of patients, although by no means all, display a series of dysfunctional character traits that include a tendency toward exaggeration and even outright disingenuousness (mythomania), hypergraphia, hyperreligiosity, and emotional lability. Called Geschwind's disease, interictial personality disorder or the Temporal Lobe Epileptic personality profile, the phenomenon raises crucial questions as to the relationship between anatomical and psychological phenomena. Anatomically, patients with a TLE personality profile display cortical scarring in the temporal amygdalan areas of the brain. Psychologically speaking, such patients are oftentimes deeply concerned with religious/spiritual issues, display artistic proclivities that include excessive writing and, in some cases, are so prone to fabrications that they themselves are no longer able to determine where fact and fiction meet. In addition, such patients may display histrionic personality traits that include the persistent need for attention. Antisocial behavior—stealing, lying, fire setting and the spectrum of more severe crimes—is also high among the epileptic population. For these reasons, TLE patients have a statistically significant increased rate of psychiatric difficulties, with diagnoses clustering on Axis II. Correlation studies such as Sperry's (1981) and DiAngelo's (1979) have been instrumental in pointing out the compelling and critical link between labile and disingenuous personality styles, and seizural foci in the temporal lobe area.

Case study LJS, a pediatric TLE patient, can contribute
to the ongoing body of knowledge and evolving question sets
in the study of epilepsy. LJS developed eliopathic epilepsy in
her tenth year; seizures appeared to commence in the temporal lobe but quickly spread to other cortical regions as well.
Her dramatic drop seizures, her young age and, as revealed
on neuropsychological testing, the apparent plasticity of her
cognitive style, made her a good candidate for a corpus callostomy, which was performed on February 15, 1979. While
it has been amply documented that a corpus callostomy is an
effective procedure for dramatic drop seizures, reducing or
entirely eliminating them, it has not yet been systematically
explored as to whether or not a reduction or eradication of
seizure activity would correspond to a change in personality
style, namely a change in the direction of psychological
health. In short, if a corpus callostomy reduces seizures, will
it also reduce the emotional lability, the mythomania, and
other attendant psychiatric dysfunctions? This paper at-
tempts to begin to address the above-mentioned questions,
in addition to explicating the postsurgery recovery course,
and its psychosocial consequences, in a pediatric patient.

PART ONE

The Surgery and Its Effects on Personality

Prior to surgery, patient LJS had a severe seizure disorder
and displayed significant psychiatric dysfunction consistent

with the TLE personality profile. The patient, an affable thirteen-year-old, engaged in compulsive kleptomania, stealing small, apparently insignificant objects from the treatment facility. During her inpatient preoperative workups, nurses observed the patient taking hospital paraphernalia; when confronted, the patient vociferously denied. In addition, the nursing and the surgical team suspected that this patient, while suffering from a severe illness in its own right, was also able to engage in psychosomatic seizure activity, and thereby gain the attention she seemed to crave. Patient LJS, according to several CORE evaluations, had an entrenched tendency toward mythomania in environments that ranged from hospital to school to home. She frequently spoke of a correspondence with a professor of philosophy—a Hayward Krieger—with whom she discussed Ouspenskian ideas. However, we have been unable to locate or confirm the existence of any Hayward Krieger, which is not surprising, and only further underscores the diagnosis.

Patient LJS underwent a posterior cingulate corpus callostomy on February 15, 1979. She was subsequently followed at the Beth Israel Neurology Clinic for four years. Her physical recovery from the seizures was good. Her seizures themselves were reduced by over 90 percent, thus qualifying the surgery as a success. Her side effects were minimal, as she had undergone extensive preoperative tests to determine cerebral dominance. However, we *did not note* a significant change in personality style, which was dysfunctional prior to and post surgical procedure. Patient's MMPI scores prior to surgery were well above the mean on the test's psy-

chopathology scales, the test's lie scales and the test's para-
noia scales. Patient LJS was retested with the MMPI two
years post surgery, when she had been nearly seizure-free
for some time. MMPI scores remained the same. In addition, three years post surgery, this patient developed an intense fixation with writing, and, later, a subsequent fixation
with religious/spiritual pursuits, all of which suggest that
the TLE personality profile remained entrenched, and even
continued to burgeon. Therefore, the personality traits
associated with TLE *may not be* direct products of random
electrical discharge—i.e., seizure activity—but, rather, consequences of an as yet undetermined source, possibly minute
or even microscopic cortical scarring. Thus, patients with
TLE may experience improvement via surgery in terms
of their actual seizures, but it may be that the emotional
exigencies of TLE remain largely unaltered. TLE, therefore, even when largely controlled or eliminated, remains
at the very least a psychosocial phenomenon, continuing to
affect the patient's life course and intrapsychic functioning
throughout the life span.

PART TWO

Rehabilitation

Patient LJS's seizure disorder was serious enough to prevent
her from participating in many age-appropriate activities,
thus leading to social isolation and poor peer relationships.

TAT scores suggested a primitive psyche with a marked fear of social situations. At the age of thirteen, her seizures were brought under surgical control, and the question for her physical and rehabilitation therapists was how to help reintegrate this pediatric patient into an age-appropriate social sphere, especially in light of the fact—and the challenge—that while the physical seizures were gone, the personality patterns remained fixed.

Post surgery, the Beth Israel Rehabilitation Team worked closely with this young patient, teaching her a series of age-appropriate skills so as to aid reintegration. Of special note is that the patient's family structure was such that she could glean little support from it. Her mother appeared to suffer from a narcissistic disorder, while her father, as is typical of this type of family constellation, remained in the largely passive role. Rehabilitation staff found the following activities helpful:

1. Role plays involving common adolescent social situations.

2. Structured reintegration activities. I.e., the patient was given a homework assignment—to attend a dance, to attend a sporting event—and then asked to rate her feelings about it on a Likert Scale and report back to her rehabilitation therapists, who then, with the patient, reviewed her reports so as to determine in which spheres and doing what activities she felt most to least comfortable.

3. Vocational counseling/early career exploration.

4. Cognitive restructuring techniques: Patient taught to re-
structure negative self-talk with positive or reality-based
statements as exemplified in the work of A. Beck (1984).

5. Physical therapy involving sports activities. LJS re-
sponded particularly well to swimming and tennis.

6. Twice-weekly psychotherapy.

Most difficult for LJS post surgery was learning how to
structure her time constructively. LJS had spent much of her
childhood and early adolescence either having seizures or
recovering from them. For the first year post surgery and 90
percent seizure-free, the patient appeared disoriented and
complained of chronic boredom. Rehabilitation staff focused on helping this patient find or develop interests, hob-
bies and skills that had not been able to burgeon in what had
previously been a crisis-ridden childhood.

After two years of intensive rehabilitation, patient LJS
appeared better able to structure her time around subjec-
tively experienced interests with a strong social component,
interests from which she had previously been barred by
epilepsy. For instance, this patient joined the school's drama
club, and, later, the tennis team. While she had difficulties
participating in cooperative sports, her personality style was
well-suited to the drama club, where she met with significant

successes that reinforced her fragile self-esteem. Important to note, however, is that, despite her modest social successes, she still displayed impulsive behavior, poor social judgment (as revealed on several psychological tests, projective and cognitive) and a limited ability to sustain age-appropriate friendships. She did not engage in age-appropriate sexual exploration, indicating either an unstable sexual identity or marked sexual anxiety due to as yet undetermined factors, factors possibly rooted in her experience with chronic illness. She was charming, even flirtatious, with the males and females on her rehabilitation team, but showed little interest in peers.

During the rehabilitation period, patient LJS displayed some disturbing depressive tendencies, which may have been an indication of an adjustment disorder with disturbance of mood, or of a more serious mood and/or anxiety disorder as a diagnosis separate from the TLE personality patterns.

Conclusion

1. While a corpus callostomy can dramatically reduce seizures in children, it does not appear, in this case, to have any mitigating effect on the attendant personality proclivities sometimes seen in TLE patients, namely proclivities associated with emotional lability, disingenuousness, hyperreligiosity and hypergraphia. Further research is needed to determine whether or not the unaltered personality style of

TLE patients post surgery is is indeed a statistically significant phenomenon.

2.   Crucial to the success of a medical/surgical intervention
is a comprehensive rehabilitation program that addresses not
only the biological but also the psychological and social aspects of epilepsy.

PART THREE

THE

CONVULSIVE

STAGE

CHAPTER 6

THE CHERRY TREE

Like squalls, then, brief bursts of rain in otherwise clear weather, my seizures were that way after the surgery. I had far, far fewer fits. I could go for weeks, for months, and then have a small storm in my brain, rain falling fast, I falling fast, and then over in a second or so, afterward the air clear, all the seagulls singing.

And yet, I still had my auras. The surgery had lessened the seizures but intensified the auras, and I wondered whether or not Dr. Neu had made a mistake in my brain when he'd split it. "Well, I've never heard," Dr. Neu said, "of a person who has more auras after a corpus callostomy, and I've also never heard of having auras without a seizure following," but both these things were the case with me. "Write me up," I said, and he did. In the months, the years following my surgery I had auras all the time, strange states coming over me morning, noon and night, clasping me quickly like the huge hand of God reaching down from the sky. The auras were feelings and tastes, delights and despairs, and they wrapped me totally for the time they lasted. They were not a problem. People called me "dreamy," and "space cadet," and my father chuckled when he saw me staring out the window and said, "This girl of ours is a guru."

Oranges, blood red and drooping from trees. The delicious cinnamon scent of burning leaves. A tower of white smoke, a dragon in a garden where roses grew. And this one, over and over again. A staircase descending through layers of feminine moss, with odors dank and promising, a single star in the sky above. The auras were dreams during the day, and I discovered I could be talking to a person like, "Hello, how are you," and be staring at this star too. The star was like a speck of salt in my eye, but it didn't hurt.

I was fourteen, fifteen, sixteen, and I appeared to grow more normal. It took me only forty-eight hours to recuperate after the operation. Nothing felt any different, at least at first. Then one day, two days, three days, a whole week passed, without a single seizure. That was different, wow! I was confused. Suddenly I had all this time on my hands, all this time on my feet. I got very, very bored.

Luckily, though, they sent a whole team of rehabilitation therapists to reintegrate me. Susie, Jennie, Craig and Chris, a team from Beth Israel, I went to them; they went to me. In general, the team tried to teach me social skills, with minimal success. They took me swimming and to volleyball. In the tenth grade, I joined the drama club. In the eleventh grade, I started tennis. I played junior varsity field hockey, but I never danced with a boy.

Sometimes my auras were tinglings that moved from my mouth to my belly to you know where. I was seventeen, but matters of sex so embarrassed me that I could only speak of our God-given anatomy in terms like "you know where," and "down there." One day, when I was typing a story for an English class, I had an aura that ended in an orgasm. I pressed the *Q* key, and heat went through me; I pressed the *U* key, and the heat turned to a sweaty shiver, and I came to the sound of *I-E-T*, *quiet*, clack, *quiet*, and each pulse of pleasure was a word, and the words were turquoise, as beautiful and complex as coral in the Caribbean Sea.

Something happened to me then. The next time I felt an aura descend, I went straight to my desk, straight to my notebook. Holding my pen, I wrote, faster and faster, and although no orgasm came, the words were pure pleasure, physical rhythmic objects that released dreams like birds from a magician's fist. Faster and faster I flew, yellow bird, red bird, and when I was done, I saw a story before me. The story started like this:

> Summers were long seasons of dry air and gardens and
> fields that slope down to the sea. The long afternoons
> were most beautiful and hardest to bear. The sun struck

everything into silence. Time stopped ticking, or seemed to. The air was a lot like a young girl's skin at the peak of her arousal, when even the hard scars fill with a scarlet softness.

Where had I found such language, such elegance, I who did not dance with boys? I didn't know, then, about the proven link between epilepsy, auras and creativity. Even though the surgery was successful, I was still an epileptic, just less seriously so. And I didn't know that Dostoevski's best moments often came during his epileptic auras, when he perceived the shapes of sounds so acutely he could have cried. Or van Gogh, who, standing in a field full of sunflowers, painted the yellow the way he saw it in a preseizure state, a yellow of fairy tales, of melted gold.

So started my interest in the arts. I bought *Esquire* magazine because the cover advertised an author interview. The author looked like a film star, looming out with her dark hair, her eyes all dream. Jayne Anne Phillips. Her stories, the article said, were "stunning," were "bits of crooked beauty," as though her words themselves had given her skin such glow. I stared at the picture and then I bought her book. "Oh Jamaica Delilah," I read, "how I want you, your smell a clean yeast, a high white yogurt of the soul. Raymond never made it with you in the bathtub, did he, soap flowers white on your high Mongolian cheeks, your lips mouthing a heavenly *O* of surprise."

Wow, I thought. *Making it*, I thought. I decided to write like that, all spike and sex.

So I did. I held *Black Tickets* in one hand, a pen in the other, and I wrote, "Long time ago, Janey walked in the dark, breasts beneath her nightgown slow as the sea; she rises only for Raymond, her pimp."

I began to dress in filmy scarves and black leggings. I bangled myself with silver. I took long bubble baths and, like Jamaica Delilah, saw the soap flowers on my nipples, which were cherry red and perfect.

The summer before my freshman year in college I applied to a place called Bread Loaf, a fourteen-day writers' conference in Vermont. Anybody who was anybody knew Bread Loaf was the best around, a significant step on the road to recognition. I said on the application that I was nineteen years old, the minimum age. I sent in the story about Janey and her pimp, a very avant-garde piece that faced sex squarely on. I was sure I'd get in. I could tell I had talent. I could see it, but more important I could feel it in the way the words slid from me, so fast, so smoothly, as though all my openings were oiled and the birth was meant to be.

"Bread Loaf," my mother said. She'd never gotten famous as a writer of maxims, and this was maybe a disappointment even greater than I. She lay on her chaise longue, and she took Elavil, and sometimes I wanted to say, "Mom, what happened to you? You used to sizzle."

"Bread loaf?" she said. "That sounds," she said, and paused. "I have a hard time believing a place which calls itself a loaf of bread has anything worthwhile to offer."

But she gave me the money. Now all I had to do was wait.

. . .

A week passed. Then two weeks. Every day I checked the mail. Every day I called Carol, the secretary at the conference, to find out when I would hear. "This is Lauren Slater calling," I would say. "Soon," Carol would say. I was just so excited. I saw myself at that conference in Vermont, in a room made of mahogany, at a desk facing a field, and every day, after a supper of wilted greens, famous people attending to my work.

I pictured editors with horn-rimmed glasses and pocket watches, and fresh milk in the mornings.

"This Slater girl," people would say. "She's young. She's raw. She's brilliant."

Brilliant were those days of waiting, those days of May, when the sky was soft, the air warm, and the sun went down in a pool of red. I lay looking for the mailman on a lounge chair in our side yard, Pepsi snapping in my frosted glass.

And then the letter came. "Dear Ms. Slater," it read. "Your work has been reviewed by one of our readers, and while she feels it shows promise, she suggests you mature a bit and apply again at a later date."

Clearly, I thought, this is a mistake. Clearly, the reader, a she and probably ancient too, had lacked my sense of erotic style. I knew how the admissions committee worked from reading the Bread Loaf pamphlet. I knew each piece was assigned a reader and your fate depended on whatever that particular person thought. I wanted a new reader, someone very hip, and then I thought of how I might accomplish this. I picked up the phone.

"Bread Loaf Writers' Conference," Carol said.

"Yes," I said, making my voice very, very high so she would not recognize it. "Is it too late to apply?"

"We have one reader who still has time to review a few manuscripts," Carol said.

"Oh," I said, my voice like Minnie Mouse, "who is she?"

"He," the secretary said. "This reader is a he. But we don't give out names."

"I would like to apply," I said, still squeaking.

"You may," she said.

So I did. I had a clean copy of the application, and where it asked for my name I wrote Jean Levy, and I said I was nineteen again, and I sent in the exact same story, about Janey and her pimp Raymond, and he, whoever he was, my new hip reader, liked it a lot, and two weeks later the letter came, and it said, "Dear Jean. Welcome."

. . .

I took the bus. I was seventeen, but not allowed a driver's license even though the operation had made my epilepsy so much better. Still, the RMV said no, first because there was still a 10 percent chance I might have a seizure and second because of the little side effects left over from the surgery. You would think an operation as dramatic as a corpus callostomy would cause some serious damage to the mind, and it's amazing that that's not the case. The brain is an incredibly adaptive organ. In some instances a doctor can literally scoop out one whole epileptic hemisphere, leaving the person with just the other hemisphere, literally half a brain, and the person is fine, fine!

Well, I didn't have half a brain, I had a whole brain, thank God, but it was split, and if I parted my hair I could see the scar, a tiny pink thing, a cesarean scratch, all glossy to the touch. My most prominent side effect was psychological; it's hard to feel comfortable knowing your brain has been halved. You can't believe you feel so normal, but you do. The most distressing physical problem after such surgery involves the eyes, which is why the RMV wouldn't give me a license. If I closed my left eye, for instance, I couldn't read any road signs. I couldn't read anything at all with my left eye closed. This was because only the right side of my brain knew language, and when my left eye was closed the right side, disconnected from the left, went to sleep. I didn't actually experience this as an impediment, however, especially because I wasn't planning to drive with one eye closed, but the RMV thought maybe I might have to someday.

So I was not a driver. I bused myself everywhere those days, to Newton Center for Raspberry Sea Breeze Freezes and to Chestnut Hill, where I bought exfoliating scrub and pore minimizer at the Rix drugstore. And to Vermont, where Bread Loaf was.

"Jean Levy," I said to myself over and over again on the Peter Pan bus going to Bread Loaf. "Remember, your name is Jean Levy." The ride was long, ten hours long, because we had to stop and pick up so many people on little winding back roads and horse farms too. I didn't mind. I had time to practice my new name, getting used to the feel of it in my mouth.

Also, I had time to exercise my creativity. I had been reading a book about how to write, and the book said you should observe everything around you, take a lot of notes, and always try to see through your neighbor's eyes. I had a lot of neighbors on that bus ride up, and, therefore, a lot of eyes to try to see through. At every stop people got off to stretch or smoke or eat a hot dog, and when they did, I sat in their seats and felt the way the foam cushions had molded to their specific shapes, and I became their specific shapes, a whole series of shapes and smells in those different seats. When the black lady got off the bus to get a soda in the Ho Jo's, I sat in her seat, and I tried on the sunglasses she'd left behind. I was in her world then, her eyes my eyes, a place dark green, every leaf a mint.

I tried on an old man's fedora hat and smelled his scalp and saw two strands of his hair on the silk lining. I studied the hair carefully, and then made note of it on my pad. "Details," the book on writing had said, "are an essential aspect of your creative craft," so I paid close attention. "Hair," I wrote. "Two silver strands of hair, with a masculine smell."

On and on we drove. My ears popped as we entered the mountains. When I opened the Peter Pan windows, cool air flowed in, and I saw two deer standing on a slope by the side of the road, their slender heads lifted, their eyes, infinite pools.

. . .

Most of the conference participants stayed in the main house, but I, plus three other girls, all of us the youngest, were bunked in a small cabin across from the dining hall and next to the genteel building where the famous faculty went each night to drink alcohol.

Our cabin was cute. It had its own farmer's porch, and two little rooms with iron beds and blue blankets and blue painted wooden floors. Beneath the bunk lived a family of animals we never identified, raccoons, probably, their claws scrabbling, the sound like pencils scratching on paper, a long, midnight story. We slept to the sound of the animals, and woke to their cooing, and smelled their mysterious fur.

I liked my bunkmates. I could have, should have, even grown to like them a lot, if only events had turned out differently. Of course the whole time they never even knew my name; they thought I was Jean. Still, they were the first girls my age who not only accepted oddness but coveted it. In short, they were either rejects like me or so completely artistic that they had transcended all adolescent categories. There was Helen, nineteen going on forty, a poetess with waist-length black hair and high heels. There was Ellie, my room-mate, the opposite of Helen, pale and plump, with soft red hair; she was writing a novel and the only thing I now remember about it is that the heroine got poison ivy in her vagina. Rebecca was from the South, and she, like me, wrote short stories.

We all ate dinner together the first night, huddling at our own table in the cafeteria while waitresses with armpit hair served us lentil soup and thick slices of brown bread. We talked about writing and our futures as writers, and, here, I fit right in. I told them about my preseizure auras, and how it was in an aura that I discovered my creativity. I talked about wanting to someday write a whole book about my epilepsy and my surgery, a book called *Lying*, I said, and everyone was impressed. Outside the day grew dark and we were so far north the aurora borealis was faintly visible, the sky shining, and on the way back to our bunk later on, an owl soared over us, pure white and looking for mice.

. . .

The whole point of the conference was to have a famous writer read your work and give you feedback. I would like to tell you who my famous writer was, but, because of the unhappy and damning events that came to pass, I have had to change his name and identifying features.

I saw him the next morning, in the barn, where I and my bunkmates went for a late breakfast of bagels and coffee. Let's say his name was Christopher, and his last name, well, let's call him Christopher Marin.

He was older, this Christopher Marin, and very famous, with two books under his belt and a Guggenheim. He was from the South. He had green eyes sunk in facial wrinkles, and broad arms tipped with hairs bronzed by the sun. He was a well-dressed older man, and the morning I met him, he was wearing a crisp white oxford cloth shirt, and a pair of Levi's jeans faded to fringe and white.

I sipped my coffee, a strong, black brew. He sat over in the corner of the barn, on a tattered red couch with a story that could have been mine spread out before him. He looked up and saw me. He squinted his eyes and stared.

"That's Christopher Marin," Ellie said. "Isn't he your reader? He's staring at you."

"God am I starving," I said, trying to act like I didn't care. "Do you think they have any Pop-Tarts?"

"He looks lecherous," said Helen. Helen, if I haven't already mentioned it, was from Manhattan, and knew these sorts of things. She snorted, lit up a Marlboro.

"Do you think that's my story he's reading?" I said.

Meanwhile, Christopher Marin kept staring. He would look down at one of the pages—my pages?—read a little bit, look up into the air as though considering something profound, and then swing his gaze in our direction.

"A lot of people," Helen said, "come to this conference just to fuck."

"I know," I said, even though I didn't. I did know, however, a few things about sex. Just because I didn't dance with boys didn't mean I'd never been touched by one. A year ago, my parents and their friends and their friends' fifteen-year-old son and I had all spent a week in Acapulco. The son's name was David and once he had taken me to the hotel room and pulled down my underpants and put his finger up me, which I very much enjoyed.

I also enjoyed that I had grown up nearly pretty. I had clear skin, brown eyes, and what everyone called high cheekbones. I wore rouge on my cheeks to emphasize their height.

We drank our coffee and started to leave. That morning

a literary agent was lecturing on how impossible it was to get published, and we all wanted to hear. We passed Christopher Marin as we were walking out of the barn and he said, "Excuse me."

"Yes?" said Helen.

"You," said Christopher, looking at me. "Did I hear you yesterday, during sign-in, say your name was, was Jean Levy?"

My heart went wild then. It did an elevator drop down to my ankles and the room started to spin, like right before a seizure. *Oh my God*, I thought. *He knows I have an alias. He's found out the truth. I'm going to be expelled.*

I cleared my throat, spoke slowly. "Yes," I said. "My name *is* Jean Levy."

He smiled. "Sit," he said, patting the cushion next to him.

"Why?" I said, my voice coming out as a croak.

"Why not?" he said.

"I'm going to hear a lecture," I said.

"But I have your story here," he said, rattling the sheaf of pages. "And I would love to talk with you, Jean."

I felt such a sweet relief then; I hadn't been caught. The spinning stopped. I wasn't going to have a seizure. I smiled at him. I looked at the other girls. Ellie was grinning; Helen glared.

"You guys go on," I said, and so they did.

. . .

The barn was just like a barn should be, the smell of sun-dried hay, birds in the rafters, poles of light shining in through dusty windows. The light fell at our feet, like a beautiful piece of yellow glass.

"Jean," he said. "I have been reading you all morning."

"Oh," I said. I was suddenly so shy I could only look at the floor.

"Don't be shy, Jean," he said.

"I'm not shy," I said.

"Good," he said, "because in order to discuss your work with full artistic integrity, we will both need to not be shy."

"Okay," I said. I wasn't totally sure what he meant, but I was pretty sure. My work was avant-garde and explicit, which did not mean I was avant-garde or explicit, but he thought so. Both he, and I, made the mistake of confusing the writer with her words.

"Do you mind," he said, "if I tell you how your stories make me feel?"

"No," I said. "I wouldn't mind."

"Like," he said, and paused. "Stirred and, and happily agitated. And," he said, "this part about Janey in the red room, well," he said, "like a I need a long cool shower."

I wasn't sure what to make of his feedback. On the one hand, my aim as a writer was not to inspire my readers to bathe. On the other hand, I could see this was no ordinary shower of which he was speaking. This was a misty shower on heated skin, soap and a shot of vodka on wet tiles.

"Your work," he said, "has an effect. It has, sometimes, an unhealthy effect, and I think you should know that."

I felt giddy then. My fear turned to giddiness and if I'd been alone I would have whooped with joy. I wanted to hear, more than anything else, that I, my words, had an effect, the unhealthier the better. My physical epilepsy was so much improved, but this is what people need to know: epilepsy, at least mine, is a comprehensive style; it begins in the neurons and then travels up, up, travels into the hands, which curl like claws around tchotchkes, into the mind, which, due to the darkness and the dirtiness of disease, seizes at colors, at tall tales, at words like fodder to fill me up and bring me close to someone.

"Thank you," I said.

"Would you like," he said, "to take a walk with me this afternoon? We could talk more."

I looked up at him then, Christopher Marin. True, he was handsome. Also true, he was old. I don't mean a little bit old. I mean smack in the middle of late middle age, with gray in his hair and a wedding band on his hand.

"No thank you," I said, but even as I said it I could feel the tingling move through me.

"Jean," he said. "Is that your full name?"

"What do you mean?" I said quickly.

"Oh, it's a pretty name," he said. "A very pretty name. I'm from the South, though, and in the South the names are usually longer, like Carol Ann or Norma Ray."

"Oh," I said. "Actually, I'm from the South too. I mean, I was born in the South and my parents are . . . are southern, so you're right." I smiled. "My full name is Lauren Jean."

"Lauren Jean," he said. "I can't believe you won't let me show you the trails around campus. I'll be free after I meet with my other students this afternoon."

Then I remembered that he had other students; I wasn't the only one. But I must have been—wasn't I?—the only one he'd asked for a walk.

"Are they, are your other students any good?"

"Very good," he said. "Some surprising talent. I have one woman I think should submit her work to *The New Yorker*."

I didn't say anything. I just looked down.

"But none of them," he added quickly, "have your power. You'll never be a *New Yorker* writer, Lauren Jean, but you will break ranks. Mark my words. You'll break literary ranks."

I marked his words. I saw my own words, then, and they had a physical presence, bright blues, shards of light, gems.

The sun was a gem in the sky. The trees were all emerald that afternoon, when we went for our walk.

. . .

He brought a thermos with him, and halfway up the trail he stopped to pour its contents into the plastic cup. I smelled Scotch. I said, "You drink whiskey when you hike?" and he said, "The sad truth is, I drink whiskey when I hike, I drink whiskey when I eat, I drink whiskey before I go to sleep."

I paused on the trail then and looked at him. The shadowy barn had, perhaps, been a more flattering backdrop for Mr. Marin. Out here, in the forest light, with the sun slanting down, with clear creek water blurting our reflections back to us, I could see him differently, and it should have made a difference. He had a tired look in his eyes, and an impalpable air of defeat. I could see how he had gray not just in his hair but in his nose too, and when he bent to scratch his sunburnt neck, a pale bald spot floated into view. Partly then, I was repelled, but partly I wasn't. In a way I already loved him, simply because I thought he might love me. In addition, he had a thick cord of a neck, and a jagged Adam's apple whose peak I longed to touch.

We kept climbing. The higher we rose, the sparer the air. I worried that an altitude change might bring on a fit; I touched the scar hidden beneath my hair and said to myself, "Shhhh." I did my ritual count to ten.

"I need to rest," he said. "I'm an old man, Lauren Jean. Let's rest," he said, "against this rock."

I pictured us resting against the rock. We were, of course, in the woods. I, of course, had come out here of my own volition, so there was no one to blame but me. Once we stopped moving, I knew what would happen. The rock was a slab on the ground, a slate altar with a worm on it.

"Let's keep climbing," I said.

"Lauren Jean," he said. "Look at you," he said. "So strong. Look at your legs," he said.

I looked at my legs. They were strong. They were also tanned. I felt the ripple of my muscles, the rise of my breasts, and I knew no matter how hard Christopher peered, he would never be able to see my sickness, and for once I was glad.

The tingling moved through me again. How is it that a person can be aroused and repelled at the same time? In fact, the repulsion seemed to fuel the arousal, as though both sprang from the same source deep inside me.

I sat down on the rock.

He sat down on the rock.

"Can I have some whiskey?" I said. I don't know why I said that. I didn't drink whiskey.

"How old are you?" he said.

"Nineteen," I said.

"Nineteen," he said, and shook his head. "You're just a little one," he said, and I nodded, and my own littleness so excited me, and at the same strange time, I knew his desire for me made him smaller still, and I felt strong. All these things mixed together.

He handed me the cup of whiskey, but when I went to take it with my hands he said, "No, it's the least I can do."

So he held the cup while I sipped it, and fire moved into my mouth and my throat turned red.

We were quiet for a while. The wind danced around. There were pretty things, like butterflies and buttercups. Then came a slug.

"Look at that, a slug," he said.

The slug was snoozing on its side. I don't know, maybe it was dead.

Christopher sighed. "Sometimes," he said, "I would like nothing better than to be a slug, and not have to get up in the morning."

"You want to be a slug?" I asked. My mother and I, true, had grown distant over the years, but somewhere in me I was still her girl. I had the heat of epilepsy, the speed of snapping neurons. I had will, too, and knew perfect pirouettes on frozen ponds, the striving that makes the world worthwhile.

"Yes," he said, "a slug."

The fact of the matter is he didn't kiss me then. He kissed me later, on the way back down the mountain. But in my emotional memory, which is not the same as my factual memory, he said, "Yes, a slug," and kissed me, his lips like two wet bars of pressure on my mouth, my stomach faintly sick while my crotch was wet.

. . .

I came back to my cabin before dinner. Everyone crowded around me, even Helen. They seemed as eager to know the matters of my heart as Dr. Neu had been to know the matters of my brain. They stared and probed, questioned and circled, all but took notes, and it was, truly, like being a patient again, under a lovely and elevating scrutiny.

"I didn't sleep with him," I said.

"But you will," Helen said. "And it will be such a cliché when it happens."

"He really likes my work," I said.

"Did he say you're publishable?" asked Ellie.

"He said I'm a—"

"What?" said Rebecca.

"A genius," I said. "He said I should write about my epilepsy."

In fact, I hadn't told him anything about my epilepsy, or the operation, and for the whole of our affair, I never did. Why is that? I should have told him, given who I was, given how much I mined my condition for stars.

And yet, the first person I was ever physically close to did not know about my history with epilepsy. Why is that? Sex itself is a convulsion, a kind of tortured twist when, for a few seconds, your head arced back, you're ugly. Sometimes, later, when I did have sex with Christopher, I would find him staring up at me, a look of distaste in his eyes as I came, hard and true. And part of me, at those moments, went far away, because I saw, however much he craved a woman, a woman was cunt to him. I mean that. And if he ever, ever knew how not only my body but my brain too, my whole damn being, could turn into froth and spasm, I think he would have hated me.

. . .

My bunkmates and I went to dinner that night, and then a reading, and afterward we sat on the farmer's porch and smoked clove cigarettes. The following August days were readings and workshops. Ellie had Francine Prose as her reader, and Francine criticized her. She thought the poison ivy in the vagina could be toned down. In the afternoons we played tennis or swam in the pond, and in the early evenings we looked in the windows of the Authors' house, where only the faculty were allowed to enter. I saw Stanley Elkin and Nancy Mairs chatting over white wine; I saw a woman named Nancy Willard with a long hemplike braid sitting with her feet up on a coffee table. We spied in those windows and Helen said, "The only genius here is Stanley Elkin," and that hurt my feelings. Still, it was okay, because Bread Loaf was beautiful, with Queen Anne's lace flowing in all the

fields, and darting bees, and the fresh smell of grass. Sometimes, as we were peering through the windows at the literary stars, Christopher would see me, and wave.

Every night he came to my cabin and asked me to walk
with him, and every night I went. "I'm not going to sleep
with you," I said. "I'm not making myself a cliché."

"Okay," he said, but each night we went a little further.
And each day after each night, my longing grew. Sometimes
I would look at him during breakfast, or standing on the
podium when he read his work, which was excellent, sharp,
and smart, and I couldn't believe he liked me. And I felt so
happy to be picked. And while I felt that his age was a problem, it was also a plus, because he could guide me down the
rocky road of Life, he holding my hand, I, for once, feeling
sure and safe and also strangely strong. I remember kissing
on a road where cars raced by, our bodies pressed against the
guardrails. I remember him saying, "Be careful of me, Lauren Jean," but knowing he didn't quite mean it. I remember
how numerous and defined were the stars in Vermont, hard
as nailheads up there.

And I, well, I was coming unnailed. I was slipping piece
by piece. It was the slowest seizure I'd ever had, a new kind
of epilepsy sex was, and the storm, for once, started not in
my brain but in other parts of my body.

One night, he brought a blanket with him. "I'm not going
to walk with you if you have a blanket," I said, and he said,
"It's just in case we want to rest and the ground is wet."

I was wearing my Levi's 501 jeans, the kind with buttons

for a fly, and an embroidered peasant shirt. We walked down the road and into a field.

He spread the blanket on the ground. "Stand on this blanket with me," he said.

I did.

He took off my shirt. He unbuttoned my jeans. He did this slowly and with an almost abstracted air, looking up at the stars while his fingers worked. That excited me a lot, the fact that he seemed not to need me there, that my face was irrelevant.

I lay down. "You don't have to do a thing," he said. "This is all for you, sweet girl."

He rubbed my arms and legs. He turned me over and traced his fingers up and down my spinal cord.

For a long time we lay there, and when he finally turned me back over he looked unbearably excited, sweat rolling off his skin and dropping onto me. He moved my legs apart.

"No," I said.

He stopped, moved up to my belly, and began to stroke it circularly, around and around, until I felt dizzy. Then he went to part me again.

"No," I said, with considerably less conviction, and I hated the sound of my "no," all flimsy and clotted, and, again, I felt sick and stirred all at once.

"No?" he said, smiling, "No? No? No?" As he moved my thighs around.

"Very easy now," he said, and he went between me, stroked me with his fingers, tiny touches, barely touches, like giving a beggar tidbits from a banquet, the feeling made me gasp, the hunger made me gasp, and my eyes felt wet, and then, like nothing I'd ever had before, and I tried to regain myself but I was gone, girl gone, for good, kiss yourself good-bye, and then hard waves rolled through my body, burning my shins, my head knocked back, oh yeah, ba de boom, and Christopher whispering, "Yes, yes," a hundred times or more.

Then it was quiet. Nothing was left of me except for smoking skin, liquefying bone. Terrible sounds had come from my throat, and he had heard it. And he had seen it. I might as well have had a seizure in front of him. I wanted to cry, not just for this, but for all the times I'd pissed and thrashed and stunk myself in public. All the times. I curled up in a ball away from him.

"All right?" he said, and rested a hand on my hip. I pushed him away.

"I'm going," I said, speaking into the blanket. "I'm getting dressed and I'm going good-bye now."

"Did I scare you, little one?" Christopher asked. "I'm sorry. I would never want to scare you."

"Fuck you," I said.

I wanted to say all the vile things in the world to him. "You're a fucking pervert," I said.

"I'm sorry," he said. He looked genuinely grieved.

I dressed and went. In my brain there was a gap where Dr. Neu had separated the sides, and in my body there was a gap, a barely stitched together rip, and all you had to do was press its seams and it would split, and then a hungry girl would howl without pride. I hated him. I hated her. That night, I dreamt of his hands.

. . .

For the next several days I wouldn't let him near me. Instead I became a full and willing participant in writers' conference activities, even though, out of the sides of my eyes, I looked at Christopher all the time. The lectures I attended seemed to be about how impossible it was to get published. A fancy New York editor stood at the podium and gestured across the audience and said, "Of all you sitting here, the one hundred and twenty of you, less than five one-hundredths of a percent will get a book published by a commercial house in the next decade." All of us looked around at each other like we were wolves. A few things about that comment upset me. First of all, I didn't like the wolf feeling. Second of all, the percentage seemed so small that it couldn't contain even a whole person. Five one-hundredths of a percent of this audience amounted to, at most, maybe someone's head, an arm or two, that was it. I saw us all in pieces, our hair drifting up in strands and rays.

I started to feel depressed. I started to feel like maybe staging a seizure. Certainly, if I staged a seizure while the editor was here, and then told her later I wanted to write a book called *Lying*, she would pay attention.

But I couldn't stage a seizure, because, since my surgery, seizures were harder to have. Anyway, I wouldn't have wanted Christopher to see.

Instead, I moped around. During meals I talked to other conference members as much as I could about my past sickness, about my split brain, and my stories got stranger and stranger—I told people my epilepsy had been caused by a rabid raccoon bite in my tenth year, how by the time they discovered the rabies it was too late for shots, and so they had split open my skull, let my infected brain swell to twice its normal size, Jesus, I don't even remember the rest of that one. I told people I came from a long line of epileptics, that I could trace my family tree back to the sixteenth century, to an ancestor whose spasms made people think she was a saint. In our house we had her picture hanging, a charcoal sketch from the family coffers, my ancestor with her hair in a bun, a tiny cross clutched in her hand.

I told people more and more. Like writing, the talking stories were fast and smooth and oh so slippery; I never thought about them beforehand; out they flew, like flocks of starlings, sunlight on their wings.

And I felt bad, because, finally, lying is lonely. No one knows you. When people are interested in you, you understand it's for false reasons, and you get depressed. I looked at my hand and saw it did not belong to me. I told myself I could not help my lies, (a) because I was a genius, and (b) because I had the epileptic personality style, my brain more myth than matter.

Often, I felt like I was floating. I felt lonely and craved Christopher. I was hollow and numb. I dog-paddled in the pond, like a dog, like a lower life-form, although I was not a lower life-form, because only human beings can lie. Perhaps

I was a higher life-form, the art of story raised to a new level of living in me, maybe. But the fact is, I dog-paddled in the pond. I craved Christopher. I went to craft workshops and no one paid much attention to me. I questioned whether I was a genius, or not.

. . .

There was a dance midway through the conference. Chefs in towering white hats grilled chicken and corn on outside fires, and when darkness came, candles bloomed inside the barn. Also inside were small round tables with red-checkered cloths, and jugs of wine, and some people dressed up as pirates, I have no idea why.

Late in the night, Christopher came in. He had his own jug of wine with him, and the candles splattered shadows on his white shirt. Days in the sun had darkened his skin and made his eyes look like chips of green.

"There he is," said Ellie.

A horsey woman named Liz went up and asked him to dance. Liz looked just like a riding teacher, or a horse. She had yellow hair and thick thighs, and she wore jodhpurs with suede pads on the inner knees. I didn't see a sexy thing about her.

They danced together, Liz and Christopher, and when the music slowed down, so did they. She was a poet and a slut, that Liz. She pressed herself right up against him and he put his hands on her butt.

"He shouldn't put his hands on her butt," said Ellie, "when you can see."

"I don't give a flying fuck," I said. "He can put his tongue on her butt, as far as I'm concerned."

However, I was very concerned. I felt a fire eating up my heart. Inside I was slamming my head against a wall again and again. Why was this? I'll tell you why. Liz was older than I, and supposedly a poetess with promise, and she had gotten into Bread Loaf on one of those fancy-schmancy scholarships, so she stood out.

The music stopped. The air smelled of hot Scotch, candle wax, and sweat. Christopher was sweating up a storm in the summer-dark barn. "Let's have some jazz," someone called.

"Let's have a poem," someone else shouted.

"A poem, a poem, a poem," everyone started to shout, and Helen said, with a sneer, "These people really know how to rock 'n' roll."

A poet with silver hair and elegant fingers, then, got up to read. His name was Mark Strand. He read a poem about a cat. I thought it was fair to middling.

"And now," Mark Strand said, "I want to introduce to you, at this joyous occasion, at this raucous celebration, at this meeting of minds and swinging of stanzas, my student Liz Haloran. Liz, come up and read a poem."

"No way," Liz said.

"Go on, Liz," Christopher said. "Give us a poem."

"Do they bring poems to the dance?" Rebecca asked. "Were we supposed to bring poems to the dance?"

Liz clung to Christopher's arm. Christopher took a swig straight from the bottle. Mark brought the microphone to her, and Liz said, speaking into it, "I don't have a poem with me, but I can recite Sharon Olds for you. I know her by heart."

And then she did. The poem went like this:

I knew little, and what I knew
I did not believe—they had lied to me
so many times, so I just took it as it
came, his naked body on the sheet,
the tiny hairs curling on his legs like
fine, gold shells, his sex
harder and harder under my palm
and yet not hard as a rock his face cocked
back as if in terror, the sweat
jumping out of his pores like sudden
trails from the tiny snails when his knees
locked with little clicks and under my
hand he gathered and shook and the actual
flood like milk came out of his body, I
saw it glow on his belly, all they had
said and more, I rubbed it into my
hands like lotion, I signed on for the duration.

Afterward, the barn was very quiet. Everyone was looking at her with wide, wet eyes, as though the words belonged to her, as though she had that power. "It's not her poem," I wanted to scream out loud to everybody, and maybe I would have if Christopher, at that moment, had not leaned forward and kissed her, full and with a lot of linger, on her mouth.

. . .

Sometimes, you just hit your limit. That was it. I stormed out of the barn. I crashed through people and maybe even tipped a table or two, but hardly anyone noticed because the music had started up again, and people were dancing.

Midnight, maybe even later. Bats with diaphanous wings darted through the air. A plane flew overhead, or maybe it was another bat.

"Stop," he said, pulling on my arm.

"Don't pull on my arm," I said, whipping around and facing him in the field. I was crying, which I saw as both an embarrassment and leverage.

"Lauren Jean," he said, and his breath was ripe with red wine and Liz's spit. "Lauren Jean, I'm sorry. You're just a kid. I should never have—" He stopped, wiped his brow with a crumpled cloth he pulled out of his pocket. "I should have left you alone. Christ," he said. "What's wrong with me?"

"I don't know," I said. "I think something is seriously wrong with you."

"Do you?" he said, and he sounded genuinely curious. "What?"

I was surprised and also flattered that he actually wanted to know what a seventeen/nineteen-year-old might think about his fifty-something-year-old psyche. "Why are you asking me?" I said.

"Because," he said, "you are precocious. You are wise beyond your years. I find myself genuinely drawn to you, Lauren Jean. And that's a shame."

"It is," I said. "You're married. And you probably have girlfriends all over the country."

"That's true," he said. "All over the country."

I stared at him. The season was summer, but in my memory now it turns to winter. The field in which we stand is white with snow. Ripped pieces of snow fall from a blank sky. Wind howls and I shiver in my skin.

"What do you mean?" I said.

"The truth is," he said, "I am married. And I have two young daughters. I am also sexually compulsive."

"What?" I said.

"I love women," he said. "Or I need women. I don't know."

I felt tears rise again, real tears they were, hot and pressured. "Do you love her?" I said. "That, that Liz, that horse, how could you love her?"

"No, no," he said. "Liz I do not love."

Upon hearing that, the relief was so sweet, and mixed, as it was, with the salt of sure rejection, I didn't have a chance, stupid me.

"Do you love me?" I said.

"What I love about you," he said, "are your words. Your willingness to go deep, with words."

. . .

I am genuinely sorry to report that I slept with him. Lauren Jean slept with him. Or Lauren Jean's words slept with him. Or he slept not with Lauren Jean but with his idea of her talent, which was, I now see, an idea overwrought and ridiculous and possibly even entirely fraudulent, even though, dear reader, well, I do have some talent, wouldn't you say?

I put myself in your hands.

In his hands.

We went back to his room. He was faculty, so he had a good room, all glossy wood and painted lampshades. Of course I was a virgin, and I'd never had extensive contact with a penis, but I had an immediate affinity for it. I seemed to understand the penis intuitively.

Afterward, I smoked a cigarette, a habit I'd acquired only recently from Helen. He propped himself up with pillows. Outside, the sky was lightening in barely perceptible levels, navy blue turning to turquoise around the edges as the moon merged into morning.

I felt sad. The sadness had nothing to do with my recently lost virginity and everything to do with this man next to me. He smelled good, like just the faintest tang of aftershave and soap and sweat.

"So you are sexually compulsive," I said.

"Yes," he said.

"How many girlfriends do you have?" I asked. Masochist that I am, I had to ask this naked and postcoitally.

He was very honest and sad. He told me everything. He told me all over the country, because when he went to do readings, national figure that he was, there was always a woman who wanted to sleep with him, and so he did. In addition to that, he went to combat zones in different cities, watched strip shows and hired prostitutes. It was sordid, he said, he knew that, but there was a need, a need, and he hated himself and if I was smart I would hate him too.

I was not smart. I did not hate him. Each encounter of which he spoke was a stab in my skin, and the stabs hurt so much I wanted him all the more to heal them. And as I was lying there, stabbed and oozing, an aura came to me— still no seizure but a preseizure aura—and it was the most beautiful one I had ever had. I heard an orchestra playing on a green lawn, and the notes had tastes—vanilla, snow, nutmeg—as though Dr. Neu had lodged a probe perma- nently in my brain, and the probe was a pen stimulating story after story after story.

I saw how we would work then. I saw my way. If I wrote well enough, my auras would grace us, their heat would bind us, and he would so much admire me that through my words alone we would come to love.

"And your wife?" I said.

"And my daughters," he said, his voice thick with pain. "Let's not forget my daughters. I don't know why," he said, "they are not enough."

. . .

Three days later the conference ended, I kissed Christopher good-bye in the privacy of his room, boarded the Peter Pan bus, and wept the whole way home. For those three days we had made love a lot; we had made love the morn- ing of my departure, and when the bus hit the highway I felt his liquid leave me in a rush, running down my legs in- side my jeans. I cried harder at that, and I was so besmitten I didn't even find the sticky sperm disgusting, as well I should have.

It was the end of August now, and the air had hints of autumn in it. The leaves were growing red in spots. I started college just one week after Bread Loaf had ended. I barely cared. My heart ached for Christopher, my crotch ached for Christopher, and I was going to Brandeis, which was only one mile from my house so it was no big deal. Why, you may wonder, did I choose a college one mile from my house, when my mother was such a bitchy and depressing figure, and my father, so ineffectual? Why didn't I want to *get away,* go smack across the country, lounge in Palo Alto under palm trees, or study with the genius nerds at Swarthmore? I'll tell you why. Every place rejected me but Brandeis, and the only reason I think I got in there was the Jewish connection.

So Brandeis it was. On Orientation Day a lot of Long Island–looking kids showed up with shiny luggage sets, and I hopped off the train, hiked up the hill to campus with just a laundry bag. I hated it from the get-go. I hated everything and loved nothing but Christopher. My dorm looked like an army bunker, all concrete and centipedes. My roommate was Israeli, an army gal, and, along with her toiletries, she actually brought bullets to show us. Did I give a flying fuck? No. "How about some germ warfare?" I said. "You tote any of that through customs too?"

I had no friends I made no friends I didn't care. Orientation week was a series of parties with watery beer and boys who were not men like Christopher. I thought of him back with his wife. It killed me. I thought of him holding his two-year-old daughter on his lap. That killed me more. It should have been *me* he was holding on his lap, me he was nurturing along.

We had left it vague. We hadn't said we were going to see each other again, but we hadn't said we wouldn't. "Maybe I'll write you, Lauren Jean," he had murmured in my ear.

He didn't write and he didn't write. Three weeks passed. I didn't write. What I mean by that is I didn't write him and I didn't write myself; not a story, a stanza, a single word would leave the crusty nib of my ballpoint pen. At last, when I couldn't bear my condition any longer, I called him at the university where he taught.

"This is Lauren Jean," I said. "I'm calling you long distance."

"Lauren Jean Lauren Jean," he said. "Sweet girl. How are you? I've missed you!"

A door flew open in my heart then, and tropical birds flew out. Ooo la la.

"I've missed you too," I said, and then I started to cry.

"I'll tell you what," he said. "I'm going to be reading in Brattleboro in three weeks. Why don't you come up, we'll spend the weekend together."

"Okay," I said.

"How's your writing going?" he said.

"Excellent," I said. And then, "I have three stories under consideration at *Granta*."

"Bring your work with you," he said. "I want to see it."

"You bring yours too," I said. "I want to see it."

We hung up. To say I was ecstatic, well, that would be an understatement. I was complete. I was a half-moon and now I was a whole moon, and the lie about *Granta* was at once part of that wholeness and the force that threatened its fracture. I was a plump and fragile planet, and the penumbra I cast was silver and gold. Ooo la la.

I sat down at my desk in my dorm bunker to write. I could feel, I could feel an aura coming on. I could feel a pressure in the air, and I could scent cinnamon. My left hand felt weak. My mouth was dry. I thought, this time, I might have a small seizure too.

No seizure, but the aura, when it came, hit hard and crushingly clear. It was an aura different from any I'd experienced before. It was a series of memories I had never known I'd had, but they were there, and I knew they were true. Once I had climbed a cherry tree. A blue bottle used to sit on the window ledge in our back hall. A dog by the name of Yahoo jumped and jumped on me, and his thick white belly fur filled my nose with warmth while my toddler heart hammered from fear. We were in Barbados, and a huge wave came, a wave topped with white, a wave that showed like a window its inner goods, starfish, seashells, a loose water ski, and when it crashed onto the beach it left behind a live shark with blood on its mouth.

I had never felt anything like this before. So much of our lives we forget, and, forgotten, the past ceases to exist. The pieces came back—at least I thought they did—and I wrote them out, rushed them out in a series of autobiographical stories I knew were the best I'd done.

Epileptics experience many different kinds of auras. Some have premonitions of terrible events, others have smells or headaches or free-floating panics. There is also a kind of aura, particular to epilepsy, that is called involuntary recall, or, as some neurologists have named it, nostalgic incontinence. It happens, doctors say, because temporal areas of the brain get stimulated from preseizure firings, and a door opens, and through it pours the past.

Some neurologists say that the memories are meaningless and not even accurate, random spurts from a hyperactive brain; others say the scenes that rush up are loaded with deep clues as to who and what we are.

I myself don't know what to think. All I do know is that after that conversation with Christopher the nature of my auras changed forever. They were almost all, after that, involuntary recalls, and thus I became a memoirist, what else could I be? But here's the rub. Later on that night, still writing in a frenzy, preparing my portfolio for my visit with Christopher, I had a memory of falling out of a cherry tree and cracking open my head, and I wrote a short memoir about that.

"It never happened," my mother said when I asked her the next day on the phone. "You never fell out of a cherry tree."

"I remember that I did," I said.

"You didn't," she said. "We've never even owned a cherry tree."

"Yes we did," I said. "I remember we once had a cherry

tree and because it got something called Dutch worm disease you had the gardener take it down."

"None of my trees," my mother said, "have ever had something called Dutch worm disease."

She was so full of denial, she's not to be trusted. Then again, neither am I. And anyway, just because something has the feel of truth doesn't mean it fits the facts. Sometimes, I don't even know why the facts should matter. I often disregard them, and even when I mean to get them right, I don't. I can't. Still, I like to write about me. Me! That's why I'm not a novelist.

That night, I wrote late. The moon came out complete, the lights in all the dorms went off, and my words shimmered. When he read my words, he would want to make love to me forever. I was a sorcerer, my spell a mix of clattering consonants, my language a series of links that could close any chasm. Complete.

. . .

Hours later, I turned out my light. The soldier was snoring away in the top bunk. Her hand dropped over the side of the bed, and before I climbed in beneath her, I paused to look. I wondered whether she'd ever done combat hand to hand, and, if so, what it would be like to palm the life right out of a person.

I pulled the covers up to my chin. Then a lonely feeling, lonely and spooky, with that disembodied hand hanging down. In the coming of dawn the room looked dusty, and my sleepless eyes stung.

I closed my left eye. Because of my corpus callostomy, whenever I close my left eye, I am unable to read or understand language. Language lives in the right side of the brain, for most people anyway. The left side of the brain knows space and shapes, but not words. If the two hemispheres in the brain are separated, like mine have been, any words you take in with your right eye only get stuck in the left side, and the left side is the silent side. Losing words is a common side effect of epilepsy surgery, and it's no big deal because we usually look at the world bifocally.

But I had a game I sometimes played with myself, a game that spooked me, which made me want to play it all the more. With my left eye closed I would stare at a wordless world, and the feeling was weird and clotted beyond what you could believe. Now, I saw my roommate's dangling hand, dangling all the more because I knew it was a hand, but I could not have named it for a trillion dollars. Silence snowed down.

I might be reading a book, and close my left eye, and see before me not words but a scrabble of black ants in a meaningless march. Or I would hold an apple in my right hand, a fine fruit to hold, a perfect palm object, utterly graspable, cool, slick and sensuous. With both eyes open I knew I held an apple, but with my left eye closed, again, I could not name the apple, or eat the apple, and so there was no apple.

And so there was no Lauren.

And so there was no Christopher.

And so there is no you.

. . .

I was only seventeen, and this was a heavy philosophical load to cart around. Sometimes I imagined the chasm Dr. Neu had cut into my brain, my severed hemispheres floating in fluid, ghostly, gray, and crying for their twin. Perhaps this is why I longed for Christopher, why, as I grew older, my longings intensified, spiraled up. What else might explain it? That my mother didn't love me well enough? A lot of people's mothers don't love them well enough, and not a lot of people develop Munchausen's, into which I still sometimes relapse when the going gets tough; not a lot of people develop bad depressions, or take psychiatric medications, or have crack-ups. I've had several crack-ups, which I'm omitting for the sake of this story's structure. I have been driven crazy, I think, by the existential truth made manifest in my flesh. Sartre says we must learn to live in space, and the fact of our groundlessness so terrifies us we flee into brittle sanity. I cannot flee, because the space, literally, is engraved in my skull. I cannot cross over. Lauren A stands on one hemisphere, Lauren B on the other hemisphere, and they reach across, trying to touch; air.

. . .

The day before my weekend with Christopher in Brattleboro, I had an appointment with Dr. Neu. True to his word, he continued to follow me, although I think he'd lost some interest in me. Or maybe, after Christopher, I had lost interest in him. Our sessions were always the same. He always had the same beard, and he was short. He was cute, actually, a cute little Dutch doctor.

We did tests. I would close my left eye and he would flash a picture to my right visual field. Never could I name what I saw.

Occasionally, my symptoms were spectacular. Once Dr. Neu put in front of me a dead fish and a chocolate Kiss. "Pick up the dead fish," he said, and when I went to do it with my right hand, my left hand got angry or grossed out and kept trying to force my right hand toward the Kiss. "That's called two-handed antagonism," Dr. Neu said. "Sometimes we see that in corpus callostomy patients."

This session, I told Dr. Neu about my involuntary recalls.

"Given the prevalence of your auras, and their intensity, I suspect you are actually having very mild and frequent seizures, so mild you aren't even aware of them. That's okay," he said. "The surgery has ninety percent eliminated the dramatic drop seizures, and you can take a low dose of Dilantin to clean up the auras." He started to write a prescription.

"No," I said.

"No?"

"I like my auras," I said. "They give me things."

. . .

We fucked the whole time. I brought him my new stories, all ten of them. He read one, we fucked, he read another, we fucked again, until we'd fucked ten times over the course of the weekend. It was hard, therefore, not to make the Pavlovian association between words and love. With both eyes open, I saw language as a bridge across the chasm; we could cross. We did.

Every three weeks we met in motels in Vermont. Our encounters were seedy, our sex on synthetic carpets, polyester bedspreads, a Gideons Bible in the nightstand drawer. Highway motels, the sounds of cars like ripping silk, he held me. Snow started. Clumps of wet snow fell to the ground, branches bowing on all the trees. Darkness came earlier then, the sad smoky dusks of December.

I showed him a memory story I'd written. Eight years old, with my parents in Florida, in Delray Beach, where malls were bright with sunshine and cheap satin. One night, we went to an alligator fight, and a man with a red cape tranced the alligator by turning her on her back and stroking the smooth belly. I wrote a story about this, about the sweetness of submission and my own arousal seeing it. He read the pages, and then put them down.

"This is fantastic, Lauren Jean," he said. He had a strange, sweaty look to him. His eyes bugged out.

"What's wrong?" I said.

"Nothing's wrong," he said. He pulled me to him and turned me on my belly and I thought, *Oh God, he wants to do it like a dog,* my least favorite position. Like a dog, with my breasts drooping down and my butt in the air, I'd let him. He moved over me, but then I felt him pushing into my rear.

"No," I said sharply. I twisted away but he held me tight.

"Please, Lauren Jean," he said.

"No, get away."

"I promise," he said, "I won't hurt you. You tell me if

you want to stop," and then he was pushing at my butt again; I felt a widening, he was inside.

He pushed farther, there was a slight searing, a deep ache. "Stop," I said. "Please."

He reached around front and began fingering me, and my body started to move even while my mind was stilled, frozen, disgusted, delighted, my body back and forth, and he said, "Ahh, that's right, sweet girl, that's good."

This was so twisted, so wrong, so florid, I couldn't refuse. Dr. Neu had split my brain and now he, for sure, this Christopher was splitting my torso, ripping me into two wet shreds, but while I felt split I also felt full, held, bound by a touch irrevocable. He pushed deeper in. A sharpness, a dark red flame of pain running up my flank. "Stop!" I cried.

He stopped, and his hand stopped too. I felt bereft, gave a little cry.

"Well, which one?" he said, his voice hoarse, almost ugly. "Which do you want, Lauren Jean? Stop or start?"

Now that his hand was gone, I felt the gap. I said nothing. The only pain was absence.

"Say it," he said. "Say, 'Oh please.' Say, 'Do it.'"

Asking me for words, language leading into life, velocity mine, "Do it," I said, and I bit down hard on my wretched lip; blood.

He began moving again, and his hand again, mythical we were, a single roar of sound, alive, while outside cars ripped up the roadway.

. . .

Something changed after that. I missed him more. Having known the completeness of connection, how horrid and bright we were, I wanted nothing less. Back in Boston, the next day, I called him at the university where he taught.

"He's not in right now," the department secretary said, so I did what I'd never dared to do before. I called him at home.

He sounded surprised to hear from me. "I just wanted to say hello," I said.

"Hello," he said, a little stiffly.

"I'm sorry to call you at home," I said. "But I know your wife's at work, and the girls in school and . . ."

Silence on the other end of the line. I needed to get him back.

"And, I wanted to tell you that I've won—"

"My wife," he interrupted, "does not always work the same hours. And my girls," he said, "could have been home sick today."

I said nothing.

"But," he said, his voice softening, his interest turning toward me, "you've won what, Lauren Jean?"

"A contest," I whispered, "for fiction."

. . .

I called him the next day too, and then the day after that. I had the right, given what we'd done. I had the need, because his absences were harder to bear.

Something happened to me after the butt sex. I started, sometimes, to not like what I'd written, to look at the words and think they were clunky. I read Colette, whose sentences were flawless, and it was just too tempting, so I slipped some of her sentences in between my own, and then I did it again, and again, not only sentences but passages, paragraphs (pages, maybe? the pages in this book, maybe? I won't say), so my work, at times, was a criminal mixture; I couldn't stop stealing the words. "Plagiarist, plagiarist," I whispered to myself, and it would not be too much to say I hated myself, but I couldn't stop. I did it for Christopher, so I could send him perfect work, and when I did, he would send it back to me with exclamation points and check marks on places that were not mine, and also on places that were. I felt terrible, fraudulent, but I also believed I needed to do whatever I needed to do to keep him impressed.

And when I wasn't writing for him, I called him. If he wasn't in school, I called him at home. "You can't do this," he said one day over the phone, "you can't jeopardize me like this," he said, and I said I was sorry and promised him I would stop calling him at home. Unfortunately, however, the more he told me not to, the more I needed to. He had a wife, two girls, a life kept separate from me. I called then, not for him, but to hear the sound of his wife's voice, a husky hello, I not saying a word. "Hello? Hello? Who's there?" and I hanging on until she clicked off, and I was left in static, random electrical pulses—crash and hiss.

One night, I woke up late and called. Three A.M. The phone rang and rang in their dark, distant house. A little girl picked up. "I know who you are," she said.

"Who?" I said. I couldn't believe I had answered her. I should have hung right up.

"My father's slut," she said, and then gently, just gently, replaced the receiver, and we both went back to sleep.

. . .

The next time I met him in Vermont he looked weary, the skin blue and crepey around his eyes. "This has gone too far," he said, sitting on the edge of the motel bed. "You are a talented girl, Lauren Jean, quite possibly a genius, but this has gone too far."

I looked down at the floor. I had so many thoughts and feelings going through me, primarily around the genius issue. Would he think I was a genius if I hadn't stolen sentences? Yes, he would; long before I'd ever plagiarized, he told me I had talent; I kept saying this to myself, but inside me there was deep shame, a terrible feeling of fraudulence.

"Look," I said, my voice coming out as a croak. "Look."

"What, Lauren Jean?" he said. "Look at what?"

Tears came to my eyes. "I need to see you more," I said.

"You knew," he said, "you knew full well I am married. And it's going to stay that way."

Then we fucked, not in the butt, thank God, we fucked the normal way and afterward he wouldn't even spend two seconds lying around. "I have to go," he said.

"I came all the way up here for a two-hour visit? I thought we were spending the weekend. We usually spend the weekend."

"Not this weekend," he said. He was up, throwing on his clothes, tossing my clothes toward me. "My daughter," he said, and then he mumbled something about a play in school, I pictured it. A kid in costume, looking out to find the faces that belong to her, but just beams of light, floating auras, color that can't be touched.

. . .

I wish I could report the whole sorry affair ended there, but no. He did write me less and less, his letters short, oftentimes on note cards, once or twice a coffee stain spilled across the back. But he always signed, "Love, Christopher," and he often mentioned maybe meeting up again.

I started to send my work out to literary magazines, half because I wanted to get published but half, or three quarters, because I wanted an acceptance or two when I saw him again. I sent work that was both all mine and somewhat mine to small prestigious journals, the kind Christopher often appeared in, high-minded magazines with reproduction Vermeers and Cézannes on their covers. My rejection notes, like Christopher's letters, were full of double meanings. "Excellent," wrote Hilda Raz from *Prairie Schooner* about a story that really was an LJS original. "This story is exceptional, truly beyond the pale. We can't take it, but please try us again."

In February he invited me to meet him in New Hampshire, where he would read with Bernard Malamud. "Bernard Malamud," he said. "Lauren Jean, Bernard Malamud has asked to read with me."

I left on a Saturday, the air woolly with fast-falling snow. The roads disappeared beneath blankets of white. Cars crawled slowly, and spun sideways into ditches, where their hazard lights blinked beacons in the thick storm. I had come to the point where I'd risk my life for him, and I saw how stupid, stupid I was. I wanted to tell the bus driver to turn around. I wanted my own bed back, that narrow dorm bed becoming mine if I would only let it.

Hours later I entered the Holiday Inn. This is comic. I was spinning in through the revolving door and she was spinning out, the she being Liz, the Bread Loaf horse, her sturdy body bending into the blizzard wind, her footprints fat as Clydesdales' in the snow. I recognized her immediately, and once inside I stood by the plate-glass window and watched her recede into winter's lint.

"Liz was here," I said to him. I tossed my small suitcase onto the bed.

"How are you, Lauren Jean?" he said.

"What was she doing here?" I said.

"I've been here since Thursday," he said. "She asked if she could visit, and I said yes."

I punched him then. I had come through snow and sleet, wind and weather. I punched him hard on his shoulder and I heard the gunshot crack of a bone.

"Jesus," he said, grabbing my wrists, you guessed it. We wrestled, fucked, and then I punched him again.

It was over.

"I told you," he said, pressing ice cubes to his clavicle, "I told you I'm compulsive in this area."

"But not Liz," I said. I was shaking.

"What is it about Liz?" he said.

I knew. I felt utterly defeated. She was not a woman so much as she was a writer. My thinking went as follows: If he loved me for my words then he probably loved her for her words, which meant my words were not the only words or even the top words, they were just words, words among many. And then I felt my words drop into the chasm, I could almost hear them hitting the rocky bottom of my brain like Coke cans tossed into a gorge.

What, I wondered, would fill the silence, the space in me? What would make me real? I had tried stealing, sickness, the lovely links of language, none of it had worked. I needed something more direct, like life support. Hook me up, please. Put me on a breathing machine, pump me full of fresh oxygen, fresh bags of blood, dialysis, cardiac cuffs, my heart has stopped, I need resuscitation.

The blue line on the blank screen, flat, and then a tiny, struggling spike.

Revitalize me.

Raise me from the things that die.

Christopher was staring at me, staring and staring, his eyes sharp green, his lashes thick and black.

I had spent more than half my life now seizing at this, seizing at that, my body clenched around air. In the old days, when witches boiled herbs and princes stood in towers, people said epilepsy was a sign of the devil, the soul and skin possessed by evil, thrashing spirits. But no. Epilepsy does not mean to be possessed, passively; it means to need to possess, actively. You are born with a hole in you, genetic or otherwise, and so you seize at this, you seize at that, your mouth so hungry you'll take your own tongue if you have to.

I sat in the motel room with a man who did not love me and I heard the sound of Coke cans thrown into the gorge. And I was seventeen. And outside the snow was coming down like angels shaking dust from their voluminous robes, a sight beautiful and beyond my reach. And I had the feeling, then, I had the knowledge. I was seventeen and no longer a concrete thinker. I saw I was spiritually bankrupt, a liar, a thief, a plagiarist. I saw my illness as more than a physical thing; it was also a metaphor, and that helped me make some sense. Seizure. Seizure.

"What is it?" Christopher said. He whispered.

And then I had a real seizure, my first big one in many months. When I woke up, I was on the floor, and there was some blood.

"What the hell," Christopher said, and then he shouted, *"What the hell is wrong with you?"*

"I have epilepsy," I said. I said it flatly, without drama or flourish or mystery. We had come to the end, I knew, a place beyond manipulation, beyond what I could handle.

"Jesus fucking Christ," he said. "This is too much."

"Yes it is," I said.

The rest I don't remember. Somehow I got back to the bus, and we said good-bye I knew for good, and I got home and I could not stop crying. My soldier roommate made me tea and, to distract me, told me things about the Israeli secret service that few people know. She showed me how to fire a gun, cocking broomsticks on our shoulders and pressing phantom triggers, *kaboom*. I got to like her a little, and when I felt lonely I decided I should love her like a sister, but love never came. What did come, however, weeks after the affair had ended, was a letter in the mail, a special letter about a memoir I had done that was not plagiarized but that my mother had told me was not accurate. "Dear Ms. Slater," the editor wrote, "I am pleased to inform you that the nonfiction work entitled 'The Cherry Tree' has been accepted . . ."

In my backyard, in the house where I grew up, I think I remember that there once was a cherry tree. Every spring it bore tiny green leaves, and in the summer red fruit that gave way to rot very slowly. In the morning I could smell the sweetness of the tree, and in the evening I could hear the bees, hundreds of them, nosing at the sun-spoiled pulp and turning it all to honey. One day I climbed this cherry tree, and when the wind blew I fell from it, diving with what must have been God's grace toward the ground. This is my tale, and I have written it over and over again, and, depending on my mood or my auras, the story always seems to change, and yet it always seems true. Perhaps that means it is all false, except that, every time, the words bear witness, and every time I feel love, and then, with a simple snap of an eye, the click of a closing shutter, the tree is gone, the love is gone, the man is gone, the words are gone, Christopher is gone, and I am standing in space, my brain split, my hands held out. If only I could learn to live here, in the chasm he cut, in the void out of which our world was born, if only I could.

I can.

CHAPTER 7

HOW TO MARKET THIS BOOK

MEMO

To: The Random House Marketing Department
    and my editor, Kate Medina
From: Lauren Slater
Date: December 10, 1998
Re: How to Market This Book

1. This is a difficult book, I know. There was or was
not a cherry tree. The seizures are real or something
else. I am an epileptic or I have Munchausen's. For
marketing purposes, we have to decide. We have to
call it fiction or we have to call it fact, because there's
no bookstore term for something in between, gray
matter. If you called it faction you would confuse the
bookstore people, they wouldn't know where to put

the product, and it would wind up in the back alley or a tin trash can with ants and other vermin.

You would lose a lot of money.

2. So, I suppose you want to know how much is true, how much untrue, and then we can do some sort of statistical analysis and come up with a precise percentage and figure out where the weight is. That, however, would go against my purpose, which is, among a lot of other things, to ponder the blurry line between novels and memoirs. Everyone knows that a lot of memoirs have made-up scenes; it's obvious. And everyone knows that half the time at least fictions contain literal autobiographical truths. So how do we decide what's what, and does it even matter? That's question number one.

3. Question number two: Is it possible to narrate an honest nonfiction story if you are a slippery sort? I, for one, am a slippery sort, but I believe I'm also an honest sort because I admit my slipperiness. And, therefore, to come clean in this memoir would be dishonest; it would be to go against my nature, which would be just the sort of inauthenticity any good nonfiction memoirist, whose purpose is to capture the *essence* of the narrator, could not accommodate. I truly believe that if I came completely clean I would be telling the biggest lie of all, and at heart I am not a liar, I am passionately dedicated to the truth, which, by the way, is not necessarily the same thing as fact, so loosen up! Something can be both true and untrue—it's a paradox—the same way Jesus Christ can be

both man and god, and when you try to sell this little book I suggest you pitch it to the public as such, jacket copy to read, perhaps, *a book that takes up residence in the murky gap between genres and, by its stubborn self-position there, forces us to consider important things.*

4.   Even, however, if I choose not to tease apart the fabrications from the facts, I'd like to, at the very least, lay out the possibilities. They are as follows: A) I have epilepsy as I've described. Ninety-nine percent of what I've told you is accurate, with a few glitches, due mostly to the memory lapses and altered consciousness that accompany the split-brain patient. B) I have epilepsy, but due to the very nature of the epileptic personality, the need to exaggerate and all that, you should believe only selectively what I have recorded here. C) I don't have epilepsy at all, not a shred, not a sliver, but I do have Munchausen's, and what you have here before you is a true portrait of a fabulist, a sick mind under siege, the webs we weave, the glistening tales, all matter turned to myth, yes. D) I have neither Munchausen's nor epilepsy nor a TLE personality style, but I did grow up with a mother so wedded to denial, so inclined to twist and even outright lie, that I became confused about reality and also fell in love with tall tales.

5.   Before I submitted the manuscript for your approval, I gave it to four friends, five acquaintances, and six strangers. All the strangers, who know nothing about my slipperiness, took it all quite literally, like it was just one more true ac-

count of yet another disease. Well, it's not. If you read it that way, I will feel I have failed.

6.   My good friend and novelist believes a book can qualify as nonfiction only if the literal facts are for the most part accurate. Therefore she thinks I should call this book fiction, but I disagree. After all, a lot, or at least some, or at least a few, of the literal facts are accurate. Second of all, even those things that are not literally true about me are metaphorically true about me, and that's an important point.

7.   Sometimes I look at my foot and I can't believe it belongs to me. *That's my foot, my foot, my foot,* I repeat, but it doesn't seem attached to me, and if you asked me who I was at that moment, I would tell you many things, including the fact that I am footless. Why is what we feel less true than what is? Supposing I simply feel like an epileptic, a spastic person, one with a shivering brain; supposing I have chosen epilepsy because it is the most accurate conduit to convey my psyche to you? Would this not still be a memoir, *my memoir?* After all, if I were making the whole thing up—and I'm not saying I'm making the whole thing up—but if I were, I would be doing it not to create a character as a novelist does, but, instead, to create a metaphor that conveys the real person I am.

8.   Sometimes, my confusions tire and depress me so much, I want to sleep forever.

9.   Nevertheless, confusions and all, Kate, I think I am a nonfiction writer, and I would like to be known as such. I record *my life*, sifting and trying to separate what is real from what I've dreamed. I have decided not to tell you what is fact versus what is unfact primarily because (a) I am giving you a portrait of the essence of me, and (b) because, living where I do, living in the chasm that cuts through thought, it is lonely. Come with me, Kate. Come with me, reader. I am toying with you, yes, but for a real reason. I am asking you to enter the confusion with me, to give up the ground with me, because sometimes that frightening floaty place is really the truest of all. Kierkegaard says, "The greatest lie of all is the feeling of firmness beneath our feet. We are at our most honest when we are lost." Enter that lostness with me. Live in the place I am, where the view is murky, where the connecting bridges and orienting maps have been surgically stripped away.

10.   Together we will journey. We are disoriented, and all we ever really want is a hand to hold.

11.   I am so happy you are holding me in your hands. I am sitting far away from you, but when you turn the pages, I feel a flutter in me, and wings rise up.

12.   Dr. Neu once told me a fascinating fact.

13.   This is true.

14. The neural mechanism that undergirds the lie is the same neural mechanism that helps us make narrative. Thus, all stories, even those journalists swear up and down are "true," are at least physiologically linked to deception.

15. When I was a child, in the fifth grade, I realized I was telling a lot of lies, and so I made a lie chart, a notebook in which I recorded, at the end of the day, every lie I told. My goal was to get to the point where I had nothing to record, and so absolve myself of sin. The first week I recorded ten pages of lies, and the lies so interested me that I illustrated them; and then the second week nine pages, the third week four pages, until, months later, I got to the end of the week and had nothing to record. I stared at the blank page, and maybe it was at that moment I became a writer. My heart quickened in my chest, and I felt fear. I was falling into whiteness. A terrible silence surrounded me. I wanted to mark the page, but I couldn't think of a thing to say, or who I was, or even how to spell my name, now that my stories were gone.

16. My name is Lauren. I go by no other. In the story you have before you, I am not a novelist's character; I am my best approximation of me. I am not a fiction, but nor am I a fact, because a fact implies literalness, a fact implies permanence, and someday I shall die. And when I do, I hope to have *my life* laid out, the soul of the story articulated at last, it is true, yes. This is true, yes.

17. My *memoir,* please. Sell it as nonfiction, please.

18. Look here.

19. This is where I am.

PART FOUR

PART
FOUR Part Four

THE   STAGE   OF

RECOVERY

CHAPTER 8

AMAZING GRACE

What a metaphor expresses cannot be said directly or apart
from it, for if it could be, one would have said it directly.
Here, metaphor is a strategy of desperation, not decoration.

—*Sally McFague*, Models of God

I was born from nothing and to nothing I will return.
The biological explanation of birth is that sperm
meets egg, a single cell divides: oocyte, zygote, bone.
The spiritual explanation is that God sends a spark
down, and the spark takes full flare as a human. The
biological explanation of my epilepsy is that a small
scar formed on the left temporal lobe of my brain; the
spiritual explanation is that God, in sculpting me from
paste, nicked his nail against my gray matter, a small
mistake, an error born of love and touch.

I have always loved churches. My father, Paul

David, was a Hebrew School teacher and a man in the bakery business. My mother, Anita Ann, was a Zionist and a believer in Aliyah. But I, Jewish by blood, have always preferred churches, because a seizure in a synagogue means disruption and embarrassment, whereas a seizure in church is part of the holy atmosphere. Churches are places for the two-tongued and the fainters, for broken bodies. Christ himself had his body broken, his back snapped on the board of the cross, little nails driven right through his lifelines. He died up there, stinking and bloody, and tell me this: Where in a synagogue can you find such a sight, a synagogue all clean and quiet, smelling of bleach and law?

The first church I ever went to was before my epilepsy, when I was only seven years old. I went with a Catholic friend of mine, and when the music began, many doors in me opened, and my blood pressure rose, and I rose too, hitched a little higher toward grace.

The second church I ever went to was at the falling school, and this church was intricate and magical, drops of gold on scepter tops, saints walking in all the windows.

The third church I ever went to was after Christopher Marin, when I was in the darkness. There are two kinds of darkness, the first so full of breath you know you are close to God. The second is the darkness of distance, of plugged-up tunnels and exhaust. In this you are far from God, and it was into this that I fell, when I left Christopher on that snowy Vermont morning.

In real time, darkness might last eight hours, but in psychological time, it can go for vast stretches. After Christopher, I felt lost. Even with my magazine acceptance, I still had a hole in my heart. I experienced an allover heaviness, and so I slept more.

Halfway through my freshman year I left my Israeli roommate, whom I could not come to love or even deeply like. I moved off campus, but I still ate at the cafeteria. Comfort came through foods, hot plates of spaghetti, the satisfying snap of a potato chip in my mouth.

At first, I would have said the breakup with Christopher caused my depression, but, after a while, I stopped missing him, and still the heaviness wouldn't leave. It got worse. Then I thought perhaps I'd lost my epilepsy, because, since the seizure in the hotel room in Vermont, I hadn't had an episode. A successful surgical intervention!

What had I lost? I had lost the cherry tree, the toads in the woods, my house, the ants that crawled in a line in front of my house, the grainy golden sandbox of my childhood, the honesty of my childhood—had it ever been?—before I'd learned to fake and clutch and seize at an unstitched world.

I was halfway through my freshman year, then, and I lived off campus, in a studio apartment in Waltham, right at the tip where Waltham blends into Weston, a much wealthier town. My apartment was tiny, with a gas burner for heat, and a leaded glass window. In bad weather, rain streamed down the leaded glass, leaked in under the sill, and sometimes I tasted the puddles, because I was hungry, and thirsty too.

. . .

Eventually, after Christopher, I stopped going to classes. I couldn't think why in the world I should go to classes. They were all in lecture halls, and I was not noticed. I wrote papers that TAs handed back with the briefest of comments, and even if the grades were good, no one thought me special. I was used to being probed and pondered, hated or loved, and the vast neutrality of college life—well, it just wasn't for me. When "The Cherry Tree" got accepted, there wasn't even a particular person to tell. I was reading *The Paris Review Interviews* then, and I decided I should submit an interview like that to the campus newspaper. I said my name was Juliette Epstein, and that I had interviewed this student by the name of Lauren Slater, the promising young talent on campus. The interview went like this:

JE: Could you tell us a little bit about your creative process? How many hours a day do you write, in the mornings or evenings, things like this?
LS: My writing is linked to my epilepsy. Epileptics have things called auras, and when an aura descends on me, I often feel the desire to write. It can be anytime, morning or night. I write very quickly; I can usually compose a story in an hour or less.
JE: I wasn't aware you have epilepsy. Many writers, it seems, struggle with sickness in one way or another. Would you say your epilepsy is essential to your creativity?
LS: Most definitely. I can't separate the two. I don't have

many seizures anymore, because, when I was thirteen, I had an operation called a corpus callostomy, split-brain surgery. My left brain was separated from my right brain, so my seizures wouldn't spread. After an experience like that, of course you need to write about it. Also, many artists are epileptics, like van Gogh, Dostoevski, Shakespeare.

JE: Do you mind my asking, what is it like to have a split brain? I know we're off the subject of creative writing here, but it's pretty fascinating. . . .

LS: It sounds much more dramatic than it actually is. I do have side effects though. For instance, with my left eye closed, I can't think of words, say words, read words. I am languageless. I have memory lapses, but these may have more to do with the auras and the epilepsy than with the corpus callostomy. The fact is, though, that I have two independent brains up in my head, and in some philosophical and also physical sense, I am two separate people, just like me and you.

JE: You must feel very different from other people, given your physical condition. Is writing one way you have of reaching out to others?

LS: Absolutely.

JE: Do you feel that through your writing you are able to communicate with other students on the Brandeis campus?

LS: I don't mean to insult anyone, but I find Brandeis a tough place. Everyone here is from the suburbs.

Everyone here is premed. I would like to start a group
for students who have an interest in the creative process,
and who also have epilepsy.
JE: So, do you have any potential members?
LS: Not yet, but if anyone's interested, even professors,
I can be reached at 931-0434. I would love to be called.
JE: Thank you. It sounds like it could be a wonderful
group. And I, for one, am really looking forward to
"The Cherry Tree" when it comes out in print.

Six weeks later, "The Cherry Tree" came out in print.
The interview did not come out in print. Of course, no one
called.

. . .

I went for walks then. I saw a dwarf. Another day, I saw a
man with no nose. I saw a child with pink eyes and white
floss for hair. In the CVS, I stared at my own face in the mag-
nified mirror. My face looked horrendous to me, all tilted
and pocked.

I signed up for some treatment at the Brandeis Counseling Center. I didn't know how to adjust to college life. On
the day of my first session, I brought Dr. Neu's paper with
me, so the psychologist would get an idea of my complexi-
ties.

I should have known from his office. It was all orange
leather, a bad sign. He asked me a million questions, like I
was applying for a passport, and he scribbled all my answers
down on a form. "Born where?" he said. "Mother's maiden

name?" he said. "Ethnicity?" he said, and as the time ticked by I got mad. I was there for help. "Age?" he said.

"Seventy-three," I said, and then he looked up.

He blinked behind his glasses, smiled. "I'm sure you feel that old," he said. "You look tired."

"I am tired," I said. "And I have depression too."

"A lot of freshmen experience depression," he said. "It's quite common. The adjustment can be overwhelming."

"It is overwhelming," I said, "and more so for me because I have epilepsy and my past has been difficult, which I think you should know." I handed him Dr. Neu's paper.

He read it, and then he looked at me. In my opinion, he read it very, very quickly, like maybe thirty seconds, a minute tops, so keep that in mind.

"This," he said, "this paper," he said, "is not real."

"It looks real to me," I said. I had absolutely no idea what he meant.

"I think you should understand," he said softly, "that I am confrontational in style. And so it is entirely within my style to say that there is no way this paper was written by a doctor, or anyone even remotely connected to the medical profession." He paused. "There is no such part of the brain," he said, "as the 'temporal amygdalan area.' There is no such thing as," and he pointed to the second page, " 'eliopathic epilepsy.' " He smiled. "I think you meant to write idiopathic. Is that what you meant?"

"How am I supposed to know," I said, "what Dr. Neu meant?"

"I'm sorry," he said, "but there is no Dr. Neu. What I

mean by that," he said, "is that there is no Dr. Neu anywhere in the world who would perform a corpus callostomy on a patient with TLE. It's just not done."

"What do you mean it's not done?" I said. I felt my voice get very loud and high while the whole room turned to glass. "It was done to me."

"We should probably talk," he said, "about why you need to tell this story, what it really means."

I looked at him, the little skunk. The whole room stank.

"I think," I said, "I am going to have a seizure right now."

"What happens to you," he said, "when you have seizures?" He looked concerned.

"I feel my hands get big," I said. "My hands are feeling very big and floaty right now."

He nodded. "I see," he said. "And is that floaty feeling often accompanied by an excess of saliva in the mouth, what we call ptyalism?"

"Yes," I said. "I've been diagnosed with ptyalism many times."

"Ptyalism," he said, "is never a symptom that accompanies seizures. It is a symptom of pregnancy. Could you possibly be pregnant?"

I started to cry. "You," I said, and then I was whispering. "You are a bad man."

The room got very quiet.

"I have epilepsy," I said.

"Perhaps you do," he said, "I have no way of knowing. However, this operation," he said, "this operation is definitely beyond what I can call credible, unless," he said, and then he was leaning toward me, reaching his hands out toward me, "unless you can show me your scar."

And that's when I understood. His hands reaching out toward me. The suggestion of pregnancy. He was a pervert. He wanted to touch me. I jerked away.

"Leave—me—alone," I said. I stood. "I'm going to report you," I said. "I don't lie," I said. "Ask anyone." And then I ran.

. . .

He was a pervert, and I did report him. I wrote a long letter to the head of Brandeis Counseling about how he had tried to touch me and how he had displayed some deep-seated sadistic need to question my disease and to deny its treatment, possibly because he was threatened by the very things his profession called upon him to confront. It is well known, after all, that a great many mental health practitioners are emotionally unstable, even to the point of playing cruel games with their patients.

Suffice it to say, I was not helped by the Brandeis Counseling Center. I thought about calling Dr. Neu and asking him for a referral. I didn't do it, though.

Instead, I tried to put the whole visit behind me. I tried to put it right out of my mind. I went for walks. I visited churches, because they were soothing to me and could possibly take the place of professional counseling. I liked churches where there was holy water in pools, churches where tiny toy fires burned beneath copper samovars, or where the priest walked in a hush of black cassock.

Usually, when I visited churches, they were more or less empty. One day, though, I walked into a church right by my studio apartment, a church called Saint Perpetua's of the Precious Blood, a small, unassuming-looking building on the outside, but on the inside garlands of fresh flowers, pews worn and almost soft to the touch.

I touched the pews. I slid in and sat. I thought I had stumbled in on a service of some sort. The pews were filled with people who one by one stood and said things. They walked to the front of the room and spoke into a microphone. To the side, I saw a cloth-covered table, pamphlets and books. I saw a coffeepot, and platters of delicious-looking treats.

I saw the food first, and then a man next to me leaned over and whispered, "Welcome."

"Thank you," I said.

It was such a simple word, *welcome*, but it had within it the delightful sounds of door chimes announcing your arrival at a hospitable house.

I watched. A woman with frizzy hair and lipstick so bright it made her mouth stand separate from her face got up to talk. I figured this was a Christian thing; what did I know? The woman took the microphone and lowered her lips to it. She said nothing. Her mouth began to tremble and tears came out, silvering her sad, sad face. No one said a word, and the woman just stood there weeping, and then I got scared. A small cry escaped her bunched, bright mouth, and for a second I thought of my mother; I thought it was her up

I have always loved the word *serenity*. The word is imagistic. It's a blue lake of a word. It is pitch pine and horses.

"I guess," I said, "that's why I'm here. I can't do it on my own anymore. I'm looking for serenity."

"Elaine," he said, beckoning her over. "Elaine, Joy, Mike, come here, we've got a newcomer."

"Do you need a sponsor?" someone asked.

"We have a telephone tree," someone else said.

"931-0434," I said, spitting out my numbers, it happening so fast, my life branching with theirs, they older and elegant, I a child by comparison, they put their arms around me.

"Seven months," Elaine said. "You are an inspiration to me. If I had found AA at your age, instead of when I was fifty-three, who knows. God bless," Elaine said, "God bless you and your time," and then she hugged me, and I smelled her perfume. I smelled the minerals in her jewelry and the hazelnut in her hair, and I remembered a long time ago, dreaming of women touching me, many mothers gathered around me, here we were: Joy and Elaine, Mike and Elaine, Joy and Amy and Brad, they saw me. They said I was special. And in the following weeks I learned their names, and I stepped over their thresholds, into their house, this house, it became my house, saints walking in every window.

. . .

It happened slowly. AAers will tell you that miracles are rarely claps of thunder; they are the small steps we take every day. I took small steps into AA, one day saying I was seven months sober, the next day getting hugged, my phone

there. I knew it wasn't, but the shadows angling the woman's face, the palpable air of sadness and something far too tight, her hair, high and sprayed; my mother. And then I, too, wanted to cry, because the idea of her unhappiness—whose unhappiness?—brings me always to a dark and difficult place.

"It's okay, Elaine," a voice from the pews said. I tried to see who spoke, but the church was darkish.

"Remember, let go and let God, Elaine," another voice, from another pew, said.

Elaine nodded. She touched a strand of pearls at her throat. "It's been a week now," she said.

Everyone clapped.

I clapped too.

I have clapped many times in my life, but this time was different. I clapped for Elaine, sad, strung-out Elaine, and I heard precisely how my singular claps joined the larger universe of claps, and we made a single sound, for Elaine.

I felt, suddenly, inexplicably, joyful. "Welcome," the man next to me had said. And I was here, with my hands beating back someone's sadness, and I forgot all about the sadistic Brandeis psychologist, and just then Elaine smiled; her mouth broke open and her huge teeth glistened, and she laughed and said, "Oh, God, I love you people so much!" Her voice echoed through the microphone, and the clapping got louder, and I got louder, and soon we were standing, and everyone was hugging, and someone hugged me, and the next thing I knew, I had a cookie in my mouth, warm, buttery, jam-filled, welcome.

...

I went back the next day. I wasn't planning to, but since the counseling center had failed me, I felt I had nowhere to go. So I just went out walking, and when I came to the church, I slipped in. Three o'clock, just like yesterday. And I saw the strangest thing. It was as though no time had passed. The garlands of flowers were just as bright. The people seemed to be sitting in the exact same places in the pews, and the cookies were fresh.

"Welcome," the man said to me when I entered the pew. He had good breath, like a lawn. I heard the door chimes in his voice, the hospitable house, and then Elaine got up, stood by the microphone, and she cried as she had before, and then she said, "It's been eight days now," and everyone clapped. Here, time stood still but never stagnant. Here, the room was filled with high, baroque emotion, and yet tempered with plain kindness and camaraderie.

I stuck around when the meeting ended. Yesterday, I'd pretty much rushed out, but today I felt a little less shy. People gathered around the refreshments. That's when I saw the pamphlets, "Alcoholics Anonymous," "Clean and Sober," "Twelve Steps to Spirituality," "You and Your Higher Power."

I had heard of AA and even seen a TV movie about it once, a movie where a boy named Bobby got up and confessed to an entire auditorium that he was a drunk. The movie had pictured old grizzled men smoking cigarettes, coffee in mashed paper cups. This crew, however, looked

different. The church was in Weston. The men carried brie cases and wore leather shoes. The women had fine jewelry

The man with the nice breath came up to me again. H held a mug of coffee. "So," he said, blowing on it. I smelle hazelnut. "So, we saw you here yesterday. You're a new comer, are you?"

"Yes," I answered, not sure what I was supposed to say.

"And how many days sober do you have?" he asked.

The question threw me. I should have been anticipatin it—what else would you ask in AA?—but I was caugh completely off guard. I didn't know how to explain what was doing here, and I thought if he found out I wasn't an al coholic, he'd get mad, and so I said, "Well . . . seven months."

This was right in several ways. Seven months ago, I'd broken up with Christopher, and Christopher had been pretty much of an addiction for me, so there. Also, seven months ago, right before breaking up, we'd had a drink together in the hotel room, and I hadn't had an alcoholic beverage since then. And it had been, most important, seven months since my last grand mal seizure, up there in Vermont, in the snow, in the sex.

"Seven months," the man said. He held out his hand and we shook. "That's quite impressive," he said. "Did you do that with the help of AA, or on your own?"

"On my own," I said.

"That's dangerous," he said. "You can get sober without AA, sure, but the program's not just about getting sober. It's about change and growth. It's about serenity."

there. I knew it wasn't, but the shadows angling the woman's face, the palpable air of sadness and something far too tight, her hair, high and sprayed; my mother. And then I, too, wanted to cry, because the idea of her unhappiness—whose unhappiness?—brings me always to a dark and difficult place.

"It's okay, Elaine," a voice from the pews said. I tried to see who spoke, but the church was darkish.

"Remember, let go and let God, Elaine," another voice, from another pew, said.

Elaine nodded. She touched a strand of pearls at her throat. "It's been a week now," she said.

Everyone clapped.

I clapped too.

I have clapped many times in my life, but this time was different. I clapped for Elaine, sad, strung-out Elaine, and I heard precisely how my singular claps joined the larger universe of claps, and we made a single sound, for Elaine.

I felt, suddenly, inexplicably, joyful. "Welcome," the man next to me had said. And I was here, with my hands beating back someone's sadness, and I forgot all about the sadistic Brandeis psychologist, and just then Elaine smiled; her mouth broke open and her huge teeth glistened, and she laughed and said, "Oh, God, I love you people so much!" Her voice echoed through the microphone, and the clapping got louder, and I got louder, and soon we were standing, and everyone was hugging, and someone hugged me, and the next thing I knew, I had a cookie in my mouth, warm, buttery, jam-filled, welcome.

...

I went back the next day. I wasn't planning to, but since the counseling center had failed me, I felt I had nowhere to go. So I just went out walking, and when I came to the church, I slipped in. Three o'clock, just like yesterday. And I saw the strangest thing. It was as though no time had passed. The garlands of flowers were just as bright. The people seemed to be sitting in the exact same places in the pews, and the cookies were fresh.

"Welcome," the man said to me when I entered the pew. He had good breath, like a lawn. I heard the door chimes in his voice, the hospitable house, and then Elaine got up, stood by the microphone, and she cried as she had before, and then she said, "It's been eight days now," and everyone clapped. Here, time stood still but never stagnant. Here, the room was filled with high, baroque emotion, and yet tempered with plain kindness and camaraderie.

I stuck around when the meeting ended. Yesterday, I'd pretty much rushed out, but today I felt a little less shy. People gathered around the refreshments. That's when I saw the pamphlets, "Alcoholics Anonymous," "Clean and Sober," "Twelve Steps to Spirituality," "You and Your Higher Power."

I had heard of AA and even seen a TV movie about it once, a movie where a boy named Bobby got up and confessed to an entire auditorium that he was a drunk. The movie had pictured old grizzled men smoking cigarettes, coffee in mashed paper cups. This crew, however, looked different. The church was in Weston. The men carried brief-cases and wore leather shoes. The women had fine jewelry.

The man with the nice breath came up to me again. He held a mug of coffee. "So," he said, blowing on it. I smelled hazelnut. "So, we saw you here yesterday. You're a new-comer, are you?"

"Yes," I answered, not sure what I was supposed to say.

"And how many days sober do you have?" he asked.

The question threw me. I should have been anticipating it—what else would you ask in AA?—but I was caught completely off guard. I didn't know how to explain what I was doing here, and I thought if he found out I wasn't an al-coholic, he'd get mad, and so I said, "Well . . . seven months."

This was right in several ways. Seven months ago, I'd broken up with Christopher, and Christopher had been pretty much of an addiction for me, so there. Also, seven months ago, right before breaking up, we'd had a drink to-gether in the hotel room, and I hadn't had an alcoholic bev-erage since then. And it had been, most important, seven months since my last grand mal seizure, up there in Ver-mont, in the snow, in the sex.

"Seven months," the man said. He held out his hand and we shook. "That's quite impressive," he said. "Did you do that with the help of AA, or on your own?"

"On my own," I said.

"That's dangerous," he said. "You can get sober without AA, sure, but the program's not just about getting sober. It's about change and growth. It's about serenity."

I have always loved the word *serenity*. The word is imagistic. It's a blue lake of a word. It is pitch pine and horses.

"I guess," I said, "that's why I'm here. I can't do it on my own anymore. I'm looking for serenity."

"Elaine," he said, beckoning her over. "Elaine, Joy, Mike, come here, we've got a newcomer."

"Do you need a sponsor?" someone asked.

"We have a telephone tree," someone else said.

"931-0434," I said, spitting out my numbers, it happening so fast, my life branching with theirs, they older and elegant, I a child by comparison, they put their arms around me.

"Seven months," Elaine said. "You are an inspiration to me. If I had found AA at your age, instead of when I was fifty-three, who knows. God bless," Elaine said, "God bless you and your time," and then she hugged me, and I smelled her perfume. I smelled the minerals in her jewelry and the hazelnut in her hair, and I remembered a long time ago, dreaming of women touching me, many mothers gathered around me, here we were: Joy and Elaine, Mike and Elaine, Joy and Amy and Brad, they saw me. They said I was special. And in the following weeks I learned their names, and I stepped over their thresholds, into their house, this house, it became my house, saints walking in every window.

. . .

It happened slowly. AAers will tell you that miracles are rarely claps of thunder; they are the small steps we take every day. I took small steps into AA, one day saying I was seven months sober, the next day getting hugged, my phone number mixing with theirs, a sponsor, some pamphlets, it happened as rhythmically and naturally as breathing.

They called me the silent member because I didn't want to talk into the microphone or explain my past drinking behavior. They thought I was shy, but really I had lied, and then gotten tangled in the lie, and I didn't want to do it more into the microphone. Most of the time my lie didn't bother me, because AA, like any disease, is about so much more than its symptoms. AA is about life, and honesty, God and desperation and desire, and these things are relevant to anyone.

I went to that meeting every day. I got a sponsor, Amy. I had wanted Elaine for my sponsor, but you were supposed to have a person with a lot of sobriety, which wasn't Elaine but was Amy, a second-grade schoolteacher, her husband also in the program, her two kids in Alateen.

A sponsor is someone to rely on, someone to get you through the hard times when you don't have a meeting. A sponsor is like a best friend and a wiser person, explaining the program concepts, helping you reach your higher power.

At first, Amy and I talked after the meeting. I didn't yet have the guts to call her at home. We would sit on the church's stone steps, and she would tell me my higher power could be anything I wanted, so long as it was larger than me, it could even be a bus. I said, "My higher power is God," and she said, "So is mine, it's Jesus."

When she said the word *Jesus*, I felt uncomfortable, because I'm a Jew, but at the same time, I felt a natural affinity for the man. It's not an affinity I can intellectually explain. In my mind Jesus had a smell; he was not entirely clean; he cried out loud, and he seemed very loving. He had hair as blond as a Breck commercial.

Amy suggested I get down on my knees and pray every day. "It's the AA way," she said. "Just fall on your knees, just let go and fall on your knees." When she said these words I thought of learning to fall a long time ago, at Saint Christopher's Convent, how that had been the one place, the one time, when I had felt confident in my life.

So I did it, even though being on your knees is very un-Jewish. I started to pray on my knees. I said, "God, please fill me up."

God, however, seemed to have different plans. He didn't fill me up. I felt good at the meetings, but as soon as they were over, they were over. The campus newspaper had not published my interview. No one called. I felt an essential piece of me was missing, a piece perhaps burned out by my illness, or a piece that never developed because I had spent so much time playing a part.

It was depression, but I wouldn't have called it that. I would have said numbness. My head felt cold.

I had a bad night one night. Rain lashed against my windows, and a huge centipede crawled out of the shower drain. I called Amy on the telephone, the first time. "Hi," I said.

"What's wrong?" Amy said. "Do you feel like picking up?"

"Well," I said. "I don't know, I'm just, I'm feeling," and then I started to cry.

"I'm sorry," I said. "This is so embarrassing."

"Oh, sweetheart," Amy said, "it's okay to cry. You have to feel your feelings."

"I can't stand my feelings," I blurted out. "I feel so bad all the time. I feel empty."

My words surprised me. They were so simple and direct, and right then things lifted a little, because what I had said was true.

"You have to remember," Amy said, speaking slowly, "you have to remember that your feelings are not facts. You feel terrible but that doesn't mean you are terrible. You feel empty, but that doesn't mean you are empty. Feel your feelings and then let them go. Don't act on your feelings by picking up a drink or a drug or anything else for that matter."

"If I don't act on my feelings," I said, "then what do I act on?"

"Act as if," she said. "Act as if you are feeling good, and productive, and, eventually, it will become that way. In the program we call it 'Acting As If,'" Amy said, and part of me knew she was right, part of me knew she was wrong. You couldn't act as if you weren't having a seizure; sometimes your body just took over, your body told the truth, unalterable, essential, clenched. Other times, though, you might make your whole world, make a maxim, make an adage, dress for the position you want, not for the one you have, smile and the sun smiles back, flex and miraculous muscles arise. How odd that we are at once tethered to the truth of our bodies and yet, at the same time, utterly free to sculpt ourselves.

It goes both ways. How odd.

Act as if. As if.

In this way, fictions become facts.

. . .

There were so many vector points, that was the real miracle. Everyone in AA was battling against the disease of alcoholism, as I, too, had battled against the disease of epilepsy. And, like alcoholism, epilepsy never really goes away, even once you stop having seizures. A seizure could come back anytime, the same way an alcoholic, even with years of sobriety, can just slip out of the blue, and pick up a whiskey sour. AAers, like epileptics, are always alert, always waiting for the demon force that can crumble a life. "Cunning and baffling," is the way they talk about their addiction, and that's certainly the way I would talk about my seizures, the sudden storm bringing me down.

I, like them, was always on the alert. Seven months without a seizure, eight months, nine months, but no matter what I was doing, in the back of my head, I always knew the world could slip away, my bladder come loose, crash. Falling asleep, I would twitch, and startle awake, wondering if that was a normal twitch, or the beginning of a nighttime fit. I would stare at the ceiling and wait.

Alcoholism and epilepsy, so many vector points. Both can come back anytime. Even more important, both are more than just physical diseases. Both are personality problems as well. AAers describe addiction as an allergy of the body coupled with an obsession of the mind and an impoverishment of the spirit. For me, epilepsy, along with what doctors called my temporal lobe epileptic personality disorder, was also a psychological, spiritual, and physical thing. AAers say that alcoholics don't just drink; they are also manipulative, need to be the center of attention; they lie, cheat, and steal from God and man; it's all part of the disease, theirs and mine.

Let me tell you, I fit right in. "We drink," the AAers said, "because there is a hole in our souls," a hole they had tried to fill with many marvelous liquors, as I had tried to fill with the intoxicant of illness, the intoxicant of tall tales, the intoxicant of attention lavished on the patient and the poet, me.

Sometimes, I know this is corny, but sometimes in meetings, hearing people talk about all the desperate things they'd done just to feel good about themselves, tears came to my eyes. Tears also came to my eyes when they talked about living day in and day out with drunkenness, with hangovers, waking up with something pounding in their heads, as something had pounded in mine after a seizure, terrible tastes in our mouths; us.

I started to call Amy more and more, not in the addictive way I had called Christopher, but in a regular, reaching out kind of way. One day, she invited me over to her house for tea. Another day, Elaine invited me to her house for dinner. I really liked Elaine a lot. She made me fried chicken and green beans. She was divorced, with her three kids grown and gone. Her house was nice, with fluffy couches and fluffy rugs and a poodle named Maggie O'Brien. Elaine fed me, and we watched TV, and she said, "You are becoming just like a daughter to me."

As far as my own mother, my own home, well, I didn't go there very much. Brandeis was only one mile away, but we weren't close, my parents and I. I had a feeling always of missing my mother, a kind of perpetual pang in me, and yet, at the same time, I had lost hope a long time ago. The pang, actually, didn't have so much to do with missing *my* specific mother, but of missing a mother in general, a warmth or a certain kind of touch. My dreams were always of women; I think they always will be, women lifting me, women touching me, women treading toward me across a pink satin sheet.

· · ·

I did go home occasionally, a few times a year. My father had done pretty well in the bakery business. He had long ago stopped teaching Hebrew School, and he had enough money to afford a fairly pricey country club, where he and my mother spent summers playing golf. My mother, well, my mother never got a single maxim published, and for a while that depressed her, but then she got a new interest; she became a matrimonial consultant. I am happy to report that in this she found fulfillment. She planned girls' weddings, from the dress to the music to the flowers on the table. One month or so after I'd joined AA, I visited my mother and father, and she was so excited. She had just become a representative for Adela's Wedding Designs, which meant that Adela sent her sample dresses she could show to potential clients. I walked in and the house was filled with white. White veils draped from hangers on the doors, petticoats flounced, skirts of tulle and satin, the whole house, like being inside a baked Alaska.

"Wow," I said.

She was on the phone. "I'm telling you," I heard her say, "I'm telling you that lilies will take this over the edge."

"Hi, Mom," I said.

"And," she said, "I don't recommend a long veil for Francine. It will overwhelm her. I recommend an off-white mantilla."

I sat at the kitchen table. I watched her talking to her client over the phone. She had a high flush in her cheeks. She had a desk piled with white cloth cutouts, which she fingered lovingly as she talked. I watched her touch the fabric samples, and I felt a rush in my throat, I, suddenly, so happy for her. My mother had found her place in the world, a white white world, an aisle of perpetual promise.

She hung up. "Hello, Lauren," she said. Her tone changed. She was more comfortable with her clients than she was with me. Between us, a certain formality. "How have you been?" she said.

Usually her stiffness hurt me, but not tonight. Maybe because of AA, or Elaine, or Amy, or my higher power, or maybe just because I was happy she was happy, a burden off my back, I didn't mind.

"I've been okay," I said. I smiled.

"Your seizures?" she said. "How have they been?"

"Eight months seizure-free," I said.

"Well," she said. She looked a little irritated. "Well, I'm not surprised. I always knew you didn't really have epilepsy. I always knew these seizures were just a thing you had to grow out of."

"Well," I said. I shrugged. "Looks like you've got your hands full." I reached up to touch a wedding dress hanging on the back of the kitchen door. "It's pretty," I said.

"Yes," she said, her voice softening now. "It's pure silk."

"It's beautiful," I said, even though I thought it was ugly.

"You think so?" she said. "You really think so?" Suddenly, my mother sounded like a child.

"Absolutely," I said. "I, um, I love the flow of it."

"It has flow," my mother said. "That's what makes Adela's designs so artistic. Their flow. In the dress, a person has movement, even when standing still."

Then the kitchen was quiet, both of us touching the dress like it was a living thing, a spirit.

"Why don't you try it on?" my mother said. "It's just your size."

"I'm not getting married," I said.

"I know," my mother said.

Then it was quiet again. Upstairs, I could hear my father dressing to take us out to dinner.

"Okay," I said. "I'll try it on."

I went into the bathroom, took off my clothes, put the dress on. It did have flow. I'd always thought a wedding dress would be stiff, but this one—Adela's special design—was soft and cool, a sheath of silk, a skirt with a small flare, a bodice that clasped me gently. I stepped out.

"Look at you," my mother said. She did up the pearl buttons in the back.

We stood together, looking in the full-length mirror on the back of the bathroom door. I have to say, on me the dress looked good. It looked great. It wasn't ugly anymore. I was transformed.

And we stood like that for what seemed a long, long time. I saw the setting sun blaze in the bay windows. Shadows accumulated. "You could be a pretty girl, Lauren," my mother finally said, "if you would just pay more attention to your style," and then she tucked a strand of hair behind my ear. And we stood staring, and I remembered me, long before I'd ever had a seizure, when I dressed in white and went skating at Dehaney's Pond, when, in Barbados, I rolled in the sugar mounds and came to her like candy: a gift. A gift. And in that mirror we saw who I had not become, the gift I hadn't given her, so I gave it to her then. We stood for what seemed hours, for what seemed days, and she fussed with my hair, and my father came downstairs. "Here comes the bride," he said. And we all laughed together in a nice way, a little bit close, a little warmth, an ending of sorts, except this: I was still in costume.

. . .

I didn't tell my parents about AA. We went out to dinner that night, and my mother got tipsy on her red wine, and it occurred to me that maybe she should be in AA, that I was doing it for her. When I got home, Amy called to check in on me, and I told her all about my mother's drinking. "Not only are you an alcoholic," she said, "but you're also the child of an alcoholic, which is very common. Alcoholism is a disease. It's in the genes."

That seemed unlikely to me, it being in the genes. Also I

wasn't sure that my mother was an actual alcoholic. She just drank. So did a lot of people. In this one sense, my mother was like a lot of people.

"So it's important," Amy said, "because of your family history, to get the twelve steps early on in life. Have you done your fifth step yet?"

"No," I said. A lot of people in AA considered the fifth step to be the most critical. That was the step where you got absolutely honest, where you told another person about all the wrongs and deceits and manipulations. You came clean. The fifth step was called a fearless and searching moral inventory. AAers liked to say, "You are only as sick as your secrets," and how well I understood that. I wanted to do a fifth step. I wanted to tell someone in AA about all my deceits, how I had stolen words, stolen things to fill me, faked fits to fill me, changed my name; Munchausen's. I wanted to do a fifth step, but in order to do it really right, I would also have to admit I was not an alcoholic, and I didn't really see how that could happen.

In a way, this memoir is like my fifth step. I am not an alcoholic and I may not really be an epileptic either. Perhaps I've just felt fitful my whole life; perhaps I'm using metaphor to tell my tale, a tale I know no other way of telling, a tale of my past, my mother and me, a tale of pains and humiliations and illnesses so subtle and nuanced I could never find the literal words; would it matter? Is metaphor in memoir, in *life*, an alternate form of honesty or simply an evasion? This is what I want to know.

. . .

Elaine came up to me a few days later. She said, "I want to tell you how my life really was. I want to do my fifth step with you, even though you're just a child."

So I went over to her house. She made me another delicious dinner and then, over coffee in the den, she started to confess. She took a deep breath and said, "Okay, Lauren. Here goes. I'm coming clean." I felt all excited. It was very dramatic. For her confession, she had lowered the lights, and small candles burned on the bookshelves. We sat on the fluffy couch and Elaine, in bare feet, drew her knees up to her chin. She started to cry. I mean, she started to sob, and while on the one hand I felt bad for her, on the other hand I just felt coldly curious, like, my God, what had she done, was she a pedophile, did she have sex with a ten-year-old, did she hijack a plane when under the influence? I suddenly had a crazy image of her, a black mask pulled over her head, her face hidden, a pistol pointing at passengers in a 747.

"It's okay, Elaine," I said, trying to make my voice gentle. "Whatever it is, it's okay."

"You're a dear," Elaine said.

"Go on," I said, because I was curious.

"I," Elaine said, sobbing anew, "I have been a manipulator my whole life. I have cared about no one, nothing, but me. I have drunk in front of my children. I have loved alcohol more than my children. I have missed PTA meetings because I was drunk, and then told people I had the flu. I missed my daughter's confirmation because I was drunk and then told the congregation I had a sinus infection . . ." and so she went on from there.

I found myself growing bored. Here, there were no hijackings, no murders, no pedophiliac sex. Just the miserable small sins that constitute our small lives. And yet her sins really hurt her. I realized my sins were just as small, just as silly. I stole a picture from the Slotnicks' house. I misused emergency rooms, I filched phrases here and there, I made up illnesses—big deal. Nothing to write a book about. And yet our sins, no matter how small, made us feel bad. Sin makes you bad. Sin is separation from God and from yourself. Sin, like love, is something beyond weight, beyond measure. Like love, a little goes a long, long way.

I went home that night and prayed. My prayer was very simple, two words: "Help me."

I was helped.

. . .

It happened like this, small steps. People say AA is not a Christian program, but it is. It's built on Christian concepts, like love and forgiveness, Jesus' words. Everyone in that group was Christian, either born again or confirmed. After the meeting, after the refreshments, there was Bible study twice a week. Twice a week we put away the AA Big Book and pulled out a gospel: John, Luke, Mark. We cleared the table of food and sat around it; me too. I didn't plan on becoming a Christian. I went because I liked the people and it was something to do.

The Bible study was basically an extension of AA. We always started with a song:

> *Amazing Grace*
> *How Sweet the Sound*
> *That Saved a Wretch Like Me*

As a Jew, I'd been brought up with a certain kind of God, an Old Testament God, punitive and judgmental, his love shown through law. My epilepsy had made Judaism difficult. It had ruined my memory, and so I couldn't have a Bat Mitzvah, which depended on memorization of your Haftorah portion. I couldn't daven—the back-and-forth bows—because the movement set off seizures. Most of all, I couldn't connect to the high, clean whiteness of it all, the stern uprightness, I stinking and dark, a girl straight out of Gomorrah.

Jesus healed the epileptic boy, took him by the hand, lifted him up and he arose.

And Jesus said, "I love the lepers and the scabs."

"I am the way," he said. "Surrender yourself to me."

"Fall into me," Jesus said, and I knew how to fall.

"Fall," Amy whispered in our prayer circle.

I saw the nuns, falling in the snow. I saw the pool where girls floated, lilies every one. I saw the broken bodies coming down, and then rising up again, in Kansas.

"When we give up our desires, when we are willing to sit in emptiness, our new beings are born," Helen whispered.

We sat in the prayer circle.

"Yes," Brad said.

We opened a book by Paul Tillich. "Our whole lives," Tillich wrote, "are defenses against emptiness. We defend against emptiness by creating masks and false idols, because we fear honesty will bring—"

What? I wondered, *What will honesty bring?* I tried to picture honesty and I saw the sea, vast and frightening, the globe-girdling sea.

"Honesty," wrote Tillich, "is the truth inherent in our existential emptiness, the emptiness of Genesis, the silence behind every story. Sit. Still. Love lives in the gaps, in the barren, prairie places."

I reached up to touch the scar on my scalp, beneath which lay the surgical gouge; was it possible love lived there, in that darkness? Spirits lived in darkness. Ghosts lived in darkness. In the darkness of roadside ditches, there were sometimes daisies.

Often, during Bible study, we lit candles. Or incense. The incense had many sweet smells—vanilla, hyacinth, jasmine. Remember jasmine? The room was filled with the smell of it, a special, secret world, this time heralding health.

...

At home, in my apartment, I thought about these things. I thought the real rock-bottom truth was in surrender, was in giving up the ground and taking to the air, like Jesus said, like the nuns had long ago taught me. We create all sorts of lies, all sorts of stories and metaphors, to avoid the final truth, which is the fact of falling. Our stories are seizures.

They clutch us up, they are spastic grasps, they are losses of consciousness. Epileptics, every one of us; I am not alone.

"How do you change?" Jesus said to his disciples. "You change by changing." Marvelously simple. A nursery rhyme. A seashell. Let the tide take you.

. . .

I went to the dean's office. "I want a leave of absence," I said.

"Why," the dean said. "Are you ill?"

I could have said yes. I could have said, "seizures, terrible, headaches, grand mal," and she would have felt bad and let me off easy and maybe even said I could take all my courses pass/fail. But instead I said, "No. I am not ill."

"Then why?" said the dean.

"I am not happy here," I said. "The classes are so big, I feel lost. I am the kind of person who does better with individualized attention," I said.

We sat there in silence for a moment. The silence was uncomfortable. I had the urge to fill it, to say, "You know, I am a writer with a publication record. Have you seen 'The Cherry Tree'? Could you get me a single, my seizures are so bad?" I said nothing.

I was born from nothing and to nothing I will return. And yet, when I say the word *nothing*, when I admit, at last, "I am nothing," I feel mysteriously like something again, ground zero, genesis, the pull of possibilities.

I felt refreshed, like I'd just washed my face with a Handi Wipe. The air on my skin was prickly.

198 / Lauren Slater

"Will you be back?" the dean asked.

"Maybe," I said, "but I'm not really sure." It was May, the semester almost over. I wanted to get a job, do a good day's work, simple, clean work, like I'd learned at the convent. I wanted to find that falling girl.

I left her office. Two years later I would go back, ten years later I would get a graduate degree, fifteen years later I would be a psychologist in my own white office, stuffed animals and puppets sitting on the shelves for children to hold. I would offer people things to hold, ways of telling their lives, but behind those ways I would offer them the challenge of nothingness, to which we must always return, that radical, far-flung freedom. I would be married to a man who loves me, but who, more important, I would slowly learn how to love. I would feel fear and holes, but in the mornings, in the sweet times of early light, we would drink coffee together, this man and I, and I would think, *A life lived well is a life of perpetual prayer.*

But on that May day, not even nearly halfway through my college career, I left the dean's office knowing nothing of this outcome. All I knew was this: something spiritual was calling.

. . .

I went home. I fell asleep. Like Rip van Winkle I fell into a deep sleep that was not normal, no REM, no snores, no bed, a slumping sleep sitting up, the velvet wash of auras, wave after wave. After the dean I went home and had an aura.

In Greek, the word *aura* means breeze, and this is what it feels like, like winds washing over you, gentle or menacing, always full of meaning. The medical term for aura is prodrome, which means running before. Auras run before seizures.

After the dean I went back to my apartment, fell into a sitting, slumping sleep, and years passed. The universe turned over twice. The sun died and then was born again, in a flare of lemons. A breeze blew, a *running before,* and then I was flying over the earth. Jesus held my hand, both of us were naked, and, I hate to admit it, aroused; we just held hands. We flew like Peter Pan and Wendy. From above I saw a wheel of fire, and then I realized the wheel was really someone's head on fire—*seizure, seizure*—and when the fire passed, and the smoke cleared, Jesus pointed to the place. The head had become the earth, which I saw from outer space, blue lakes for eyes, red clay skin, so gorgeous I cried.

I opened my eyes. Or maybe I had never closed them. Or maybe I had actually had a seizure, because I did have a headache and my mouth was dry. Sometimes it's hard to tell the difference between the prodrome and a very small seizure. In any case, it didn't matter. It was physical but spiritual. God had visited me. He was here.

. . .

I had an appointment with Dr. Neu. "No seizures, but auras," I said.

"Or very small seizures," he said, "that's what I think,

but the point is, you're not having grand mal, and it's not getting in the way of your functioning." He paused. "Or is it?" he said. "How is your functioning?"

"I am changing," I said. "For the first time in my life I feel like I'm actually starting to function well."

"How's that?" he said.

"Well," I said, and then I got embarrassed. It's hard to talk about religious things in our society. "I guess," I said. "In my auras," I said, "I'm sometimes seeing God. Don't take that the wrong way, it's not like I think I'm God or anything, but I have the feeling God is close to me."

We were sitting in his office. He suddenly looked very interested. He leaned forward in his seat.

"Like how?" he said.

I didn't tell him about AA, but I did tell him about Bible study, the prayer circle, my feeling of being drawn to churches, my memories of the convent at Saint Christopher's coming back, and this desire I had to read the words of Jesus.

"That's the TLE personality," he said. "There it is again."

"What do you mean?" I said.

"Epileptics," he said, "are often drawn to creative and religious pursuits. There seems to be something about the neural discharge that lends itself to these states. There was," he said, "Saint Teresa of Avila, Saint Paul, Moses, you know, Mohammed, the prophet Ezekiel." He paused. He looked genuinely excited. "Epilepsy," he said, "is truly fascinating.

Over and over again I am awed to see how consistently my TLE patients display the same symptoms."

First, I felt flattered. I mean, it's hard not to feel good being put in the same class as Moses and Mohammed. I looked out the office window and waited to see if the bushes would start to burn. However, they didn't. They stayed stubbornly, resolutely, bushes.

"Amazing," Dr. Neu murmured.

Then I got mad. "Do you mean to tell me," I said, "that my spiritual feelings are just symptoms of a disease? I don't think so," I said.

"Look," he said. "It's not an either/or thing. Who knows, maybe the disease is God's way of reaching certain people; God causes the disease, the disease gives way to God. Who knows?"

"Who knows?" I said, but I still felt angry. "You know," I said, "you know, Dr. Neu, all those seizures I had right before the operation? I brought a lot of them on myself, because I liked the attention. I think I fooled you. I went to the library and read books about seizures and said I had a lot of symptoms that I never really had."

"That doesn't surprise me," he said. "Exaggeration, trickery, we know that's part of your personality profile. I suspected all along you were hamming things up a bit."

His demeanor disturbed me. He seemed utterly unfazed. "I lied," I said, my voice rising, a bit righteously I might add. "I lied and a lie is a sin and a sin is never small, because it's a form of separation from God."

202 / Lauren Slater

"Okay," he said, "you lied. But really, Lauren, I don't want you to feel guilty. In one sense you lied, but in another sense you didn't, because trickery is so hinged to your personality style, and, therefore, you were only being true to yourself."

. . .

Well, he was right, but I was still mad. I felt like that visit diminished me. I lost a little bit of faith. Here, I'd dropped out of school and was going to live cleanly and honestly and close to the spiritual pulse of things, and maybe that was all just chemical. Maybe none of it mattered.

I went to an AA meeting that afternoon, but I couldn't connect. Depression came back. I filled my mouth with butter cookies.

I was so easily derailed in those days, just like an alcoholic, newly sobered, can sink straight into a drink.

I had tastes in my mouth, tastes like vodka and gin. My stomach felt sick. At the meeting they lit incense and the incense smelled of piss.

I pulled a prayer book out from the wooden pocket of the pew. I opened it and closed my right eye. With my left eye, I watched the meaningless march of words, surgically shattered.

"Newcomers speak," someone said.

I looked up. I opened both eyes and looked up.

"It's newcomers' night," Helen said. "We dedicate this microphone to the stories of those new to sobriety or new to the program itself."

I was sitting next to Brad. "Go on," he said. He elbowed me. "Why don't you speak? You're new to the program and so far you haven't done a drunk-a-logue."

Drunk-a-logue was the word AAers used to describe what they did up there, in the microphone. They told the woeful tales of their drinking days; they repented in front of everyone.

"No," I said. "Not now."

"Go on," Brad said. He was speaking loudly. He even gave me a little shove, the jerk.

Amy turned from the front pew. "Lauren," she said, "I think it's your time. I think it's time."

And before I knew it everyone was saying, "Go on, Lauren, tell us your tale, Lauren, the story saves, Lauren," and the incense smelled like piss, my mouth pinging with phantom spirits, I felt bad, because of Dr. Neu, or maybe just a seizure, a physical thing, and Jesus flying far above me, as small as a mosquito in the sky, I could not connect.

And I was wafted up there, a breeze blew me up there, the voices a kind of aura carrying me, *running before, standing before*, them. Them. And the microphone, it looked like, like a microphone, a device to deepen my voice.

This, I thought, was my chance to tell the truth. They wanted my story, I would tell them my story. I was not an alcoholic, I suffered from a different disease. I had told them I was an alcoholic because in some deep sense it seemed true. Alcoholism can stand in for epilepsy, the same way epilepsy can stand in for depression, for disintegration, for self-hatred, for the unspeakable dirt between a mother and a daughter; sometimes you just don't know how to say the pain directly—I do not know how to say the pain directly, I never have—and I often tell myself it really doesn't matter, because either way, any way, the brain shivers and craves, cracked open.

And yet there is always the desire to find the words that refer directly to reality, fact and truth together. I wanted to try. Try. My heart pounded. I can come up with no better phrase. My heart was a huge hammer pounding, pounding on nothing but my blood. My blood splashed around. I thought I would faint. "Tell your tale, Lauren," and I saw my tale, and God, I wanted to tell it *as it really was* and have them love me, have them listen to me still. That is all we ever want, the one risk we're too afraid to take.

A fly landed on the rim of the microphone, black with sheer wings. I watched it crawl over the pores and the sound of its tiny tread filled the room, *crackle*.

I couldn't. I felt lost. I felt frightened. It's hard to break old habits. I relapsed, just like an alcoholic. I said:

"My name is Lauren."

"Hello, Lauren," everyone answered.

"And I am an alcoholic," I said. I started to cry.

"You're brave," someone said. "Admitting the truth is the bravest, most healing thing."

"I have never been able to admit or even know the truth," I continued. I took a deep breath. "It's part of my disease. I had my first drink, what I mean by that is my disease began, when I was ten years old. We were in Barbados, and my mother, she was an alcoholic, and she was drinking a lot. It was night, New Year's Eve, and I remember all the lights and the sound of the ocean crashing. And my mother got very drunk, insulting people and showing off at the piano. And a great sadness but also a great pride filled me, and somehow, I link my disease to these two emotions: sadness and pride. And my mother."

I paused. My tears dried. My voice got smooth and confident. I felt the story take shape, and it really was true; it flew from me.

"After that first episode," I said, "my disease got worse. I started, you know, doing it at home, in school, all the time, just stumbling around and making a real fool of myself. When I think back on my behavior now, I am humiliated. Just humiliated. But I couldn't control myself then, and I can't even really control myself now; all I remember is stumbling, and tripping, and the stink. I remember the stink."

I lowered my gaze. I looked back up.

"The stink," I said, "of my sickness.

"My parents were beside themselves, even though, well, my mother was just as sick, you know? But they focused on me. That's what happens in dysfunctional families, one person gets focused on and absorbs all the craziness. I was that person. They sent me away. I went to a hospital-like place in Kansas, where nurses and nuns tried to help me out. Nuns taught me how to cope with life, how to be strong and practical, by scrubbing floors, by washing windows and baking bread; it was therapy. And it helped. I loved those nuns. I first felt God in their presence."

"Amen," someone said.

My voice rose, a choir of confidence.

"And you know what? When I got home from this school I was better for a while, but then, the disease . . . It's a disease of—"

I stopped. Everyone was looking at me. I had them in my hands. I felt this was the best drunk-a-logue anyone had ever done. It wasn't what I was saying, but how I was saying it, my voice so genuine, so painful, so utterly, absolutely authentic, and it was! It was!

It wasn't!

"It's a disease of what?" I shouted. I felt the fire in me.

"It's cunning and baffling," someone said.

"What else?" I shouted, my mouth right up against the microphone.

"Of physical and spiritual anguish," someone else shouted out.

"People," I said. I lowered my voice and the audience lowered with me. We all went down, tight together, woven in the strands of my story.

"People, it's a disease of relapse. Relapse!" I said, "And that's what happened to me after I came back from the convent. I relapsed, I became an adolescent, and my disease progressed. I started stealing. I walked right into my neighbors' houses and stole, and let me tell you this. It is worse, spiritually speaking, to steal from a neighbor than to steal from a store, even if you take your neighbor's toilet paper. Because the Bible says to love your neighbor, but it doesn't say to love your stores."

I paused and looked around me again. Someone tittered.

The stained glass windows seemed to be glowing with a preternatural brightness; red, rose, lime. I lifted.

"I stole from my neighbors and then, later on, I stole from books, lifted words and phrases. And I was such a lonely, needy kid that instead of hiding my disease like a lot of alcoholics do, I showed it off. You people," I said. "You people talk about hiding your whiskey bottles, your martini glasses, your slurring words; well, I didn't. I made sure everyone saw, and even when I wasn't having an episode I pretended I was. I know that sounds weird, to exaggerate your disease, to entirely *create* your disease, but that's what happened. Even when I was sober, I stumbled and slurred and went into emergency rooms, and in this way I learned how to talk to the world and to hide from it, both at the same time. Showing off," I said, "is itself a kind of hiding."

I paused to let my words sink in.

"The clown is the loneliest person," I said.

"The brighter the clothes," I said, "the more somber the soul.

"I hid," I said, "through lies, but at the same time, every tale I told expressed a truth. It has been very confusing for me."

I stopped.

The room was dead quiet. "What is sobriety?" I said. "It's not limited to alcohol, it's a whole life concept that can apply to everyone. Therefore, I can be in AA whether I drink or don't because AA is about the sober soul. This," I said, "this is what you people have helped me with. You have given me a way to tell my tale, but at the same time you have shown me how to sit with emptiness, and it's been very very difficult for me.

"You don't need the details," I said. "You don't need all the little niggling facts. You don't need to know that I drank this on one night, that on another, because those facts are irrelevant. The only thing that's relevant is that I have a disease—no, that I have *the* disease, and I am here to be healed.

"Help me."

Everyone clapped like crazy and cried, even the men. "Oh my God," they said, "that was so honest."

Inside of me, my heart crashed off a cliff again and again; girl gone, Gomorrah.

. . .

I went home and poured myself some wine. I told myself I'd spoken 99.9 percent correctly, except that I was describing another disease, so I shouldn't feel bad, but I felt very bad. I told myself that the figurative truth means more than the literal truth, but I still felt bad. I felt like a liar. I loved Elaine. I loved Amy. I loved Brad and Sue and Anne and Mike. My friends. And yet I was surrounded by smoke.

I poured myself a glass of red wine. In the clear goblet, the drink blazed like a tulip.

I drank the wine, and then I had more, and then more still, but I could not, would not, get drunk. My aim was to get drunk so I could make my tale true retrospectively at least. However, I stayed stubbornly sober. My body seemed to be telling me *Here, here is the truth, truth begins in the body, and the body is made by God.*

I looked at my hand. Sometimes, one of the symptoms of epilepsy is the sense that a piece of your body does not belong to you. I held up my hand, though, and saw for sure it was mine.

"This is my hand," I said.

I once read that fact is the basis of all morality. Part of me had always pooh-poohed that, because anyone with depth knows the emotional truth means so much more.

And yet, sitting there, I felt a fact in me. For the first time, maybe ever in my life, I felt I had a definite fact, and the fact was in my stomach, solid and soft both, a stone with a shape I could see; I could see! I can see! And this is what I saw:

A half-empty wine bottle.
A goblet bright as a tulip.
She is not an alcoholic.
I am not an alcoholic.
Now tell.

I decided to proceed as follows. I felt a firm orientation, knowing what I was not. I blinked and looked around. It was June, then, and the early roses were fluffing out, and clouds with clear outlines sailed across the sky.

Each slat in each picket fence seemed so separate, so freshly white.

Our AA group had planned a weekend retreat to a monastery in New Hampshire, a Franciscan monastery where hooded brothers would lead us in prayer and contemplation. There would be services in a country church, small stone rooms with narrow beds, no excess anywhere, a world of pure *is*.

I would tell on that weekend retreat. My diseased brain is a series of crisscrossed nerves and mismatched signals, of auras that perpetually blend. And my personality, for reasons physical and other, makes that blending even worse by the need to boast and fib till the cows come home. Well here, at this country monastery, the cows were coming home. Since my drunk-a-logue, for the first time in my life I felt clear, like God had washed my eyes with Windex, I saw what I was not, and I saw that the self is forever surrounded by the loneliest smoke unless it can tell its true tale. I saw I loved Elaine, and Amy, and God himself, and that every intimacy is eroded by any deceit.

I lived alone in a studio apartment. I missed the world.

I packed a weekend bag.

We drove up there in a van. Elaine sat on one side of me, Amy on the other, and we ate popcorn. We went over a bridge and deep beneath us a river swept over rocks, sent spray into the air. I leaned my head out the window and felt each distinct drop hit my face, moisten my lips, touch my tongue: tell.

That night, over dinner, Brother Joseph read us a story. Afterward, we went into the den for our AA group. "What's wrong, sweetie?" Elaine said. "You look upset."

My palms felt clammy. How do you say to an AA group

that you've been, well, that you don't have the very disease you've led them to believe you have? How do you say that after they've told you what an inspiration you are, how totally honest you are; I wanted them to love me.

I wanted them to say, *Okay*.

Inside of me, I felt my fact. I felt the smooth stone washed by the river of God, bright blue in my stomach.

It grew dark. We lit a fire, sat in the den. Instead of using a podium format, we went around in a circle. People spoke about gratefulness and relapse and fearless and searching moral inventories. When it was Elaine's turn she said, "I did my fifth step a few weeks ago with Lauren. Lauren is special. There is something in the way she listens. You feel she is taking you in. You feel cleansed."

Everyone looked at me. I shrugged.

"Since Lauren's drunk-a-logue," Brad said, "I have felt newly sober. I have been reminded of my priorities, which have to do with articulating experience."

It was my turn then. I was so scared I lost my whole body. I could feel only my mouth, my tongue, huge and glowing in the darkened room.

"Look," I said, and I pictured my tongue flickering, fat. "I want to thank everyone in this group for their support. I want to thank everyone in this group for being so accepting. I am hoping that after I tell you what I have to tell you tonight, you will accept me still."

It was so quiet then, I could hear only the fire crackling in the fireplace, each flame forked.

"I don't," I said, "I don't really have a drinking problem.

I don't think I am really an alcoholic, I don't have that disease, I'm sorry, I've been confused, but I'm sure, I'm sure,
I'm really not an alcoholic my life has been difficult in so
many ways except I really *really* don't drink in a problematic
way I don't and I've been needing to say this out—"

"Shhh," Brad said, putting his hand on my shoulder.

Elaine came over and knelt by me. "We see this all the
time," she said.

"It was too soon," Amy said. "We shouldn't have pushed
you to do that drunk-a-logue. You're too early in recovery.
Too much truth can overwhelm a person."

"I'm not overwhelmed," I said. "I'm just not an alcoholic."

"Denial," Elaine said, squeezing next to me on the sofa.
"Denial always kicks in when we get too close to the truth."

"No," I said.

"Shhh," she said.

"Shhh, shhh, shhh," everyone was saying, everyone
leaning in toward me, their faces stained and dripping with
firelight, their shushing sounds soft and comforting, blurry
and rocking. I leaned back into them. I leaned on someone's
shoulder. Silk. The stone in my stomach turned to silk, and
then melted away. I thought, *Well, maybe I am an alcoholic,
after all the AAers say my mother is and Amy said it's a question
of genes, the other night I did drink too much, didn't I, haven't
I, I could be,* I got confused, and my fact blew away, and I
found myself back in the world I knew best, the strange
warped world, a world of so many stories—I am an alco-

holic I am not an alcoholic; I am an epileptic I am not an epileptic—a world peopled with princes, with color, with cities of salt and perpetual, perpetual possibilities, plots unfolding one into the other, *I could be I might be, and there are so many ways to tell a tale;* oh, said Shakespeare, oh what webs we weave.

And I leaned into the web, which the spider of my soul made for me. Spiders are ugly, lonely creatures. They make webs and live in that lace like spinsters, live in that lace lonely. "Shhh," everyone was saying, "you're in denial," everyone was saying, and I felt grateful that nothing would change, and then I felt furious, I mean *furious* that nothing would ever, ever change for me, that I would never land on the literal, that I would never maintain to them, "I am not an alcoholic," or to you, "I am not an epileptic, I am *really really* not an epileptic, I've had many problems in my life, but epilepsy has not been one of them." Even if I wanted to tell you this (and I do not want to tell you this; fall with me, please), I could not maintain my claim to you, because you would probably question me and say, "You mean after all this you've *never* had a seizure?" and then I would lose my ground and say, "Well, my whole life has been a seizure, I have a fitful, restless brain, I feel I have several selves, I have had many serious psychiatric and neurological problems, and even if there was no Kansas, and even if there were no nuns, there were many nurses—women in white, women in white—tall tales, the truest way I know, and Sartre, who says the metaphorical world and the material world blend

214 / Lauren Slater

and blur, become each other; believe me, I have suffered seizures."

And I looked at the AAers whom I had tried to tell, because the burden of living in limbo, of never coming down, clean and hard like a hammer on the nail of absolute knowing, was at once just too heavy and just too tempting. And so I looked at those AAers who would not hear me. They would not hear me! There they were with their solid, sure faces, everyone dripping like demons with firelight, they were so damn cocky, they with their solid little steps, their maps and rules, a fucking cult they were. "Shhh," they said. "You're in denial," they said.

Somewhere, a door slammed shut in me. A child screamed, temper tantrum. "Look," I said, but their empathy drowned me out. "I have to go," I said, and I stood. I don't remember what happened next. I felt hate. Is that a fact? I felt hate. I ran out of the room.

. . .

In the fourteenth century the fact was that the world was flat; we now know for a fact it's round. We once knew for a fact that the sun and the stars and all the other planets orbited the earth, which was a pearl, a throne in the center of the entire sky. Aristotle announced that if a couple copulated facing north or south, a boy would be born; east or west for a girl. Now we know that's not true, but for a fact, sex prior to ovulation makes a female, during makes a male; we can control. Take salts and your skin diseases will go away; a pink bath helps you breathe. Epilepsy today is definitely a physical thing, but two hundred years ago it was definitely a demon. You can be cured, today, with drugs, but long ago the same cure came through stork's dung, the liver of a she-goat, an amulet of stones taken from the stomach of a swallow at the waxing moon.

. . .

I went outside. I walked far, far into a field. I had anger in me. I had no facts, only fictions. When I turned, the lit windows of the monastery were tiny as the tips of stars.

In Boolean math, 1 plus 1 does not equal 2. It equals 10. In Riemann geometrics, the shortest distance between two points is not necessarily a straight line.

When I die, and am judged, either by myself or by the spirit that seeps through the universe, what will be said? Will I be considered brave for the fog I've tolerated, or too cowardly to face the bright light of truth, or, simply, too crippled, my brain too broken? It's not my fault, I say.

If it is not my fault, if I cannot even claim my own faults, the splits in the center of my skull, then I really have given myself away.

It is my fault. This is something I can claim. My fault. My split. My guilt. Here. Here is where I am.

Thus, myself. My memoir, please. Nonfiction, please.

I laughed out loud, then.

An owl answered me.

I was alone, in a far, far field, and then I walked farther, and the monastery disappeared.

It started snowing, even though the season was summer,

and all the flowers were in bloom. Snow fell on the flowers—the wild roses, the dark berry bushes, the purple peonies, the Queen Anne's lace, snowdrops and lemon drops, and then the universe turned over twice. A great hole opened up in the ground, a hole that Lewis Carroll himself had dug. He was an epileptic, and when he wrote about Alice dropping down the hole, we know he was really writing his own memoir, the disease sucking all solidity away. You could just cry over that. You could just cry and seize at whatever solid shreds there are, but isn't that the biggest lie of all? The world is flat. The world is round. East, west, north, south, it's always changing; clutch at what? You tell me.

Like this. You throw your legs out at the hip and give in. You say "snow," and turn into snow. You give up the ground, which you never really had to begin with, and something else takes over, and that something, with or without a face, beyond proof or even theory, that's the one fact I will ever and only have. I have the fact of falling, this is a story, finally, of falling, thank you Sister Julia, thank you Sister Patricia, I can stop seizing now; so can you. Open your fists. Go girl. Cheer for me madly. I will not win. If I am on a horse, we will both fall into the hole. If I am a gymnast, I will miss my mark, and fall, in my pale blue leotard, straight into the hole. Alice is there. The queen is there. My mother is there. Oh, Mom, I miss you. Give me a kiss good-bye. Cheer for me madly. Out in that field, I heard it happening. The trees cheered, the stars cheered, the monks and nuns and friends and family cheered as I went down, legs hurled out at the hip, I fell, and gave up the ground, and for that split second, spinning in utter space, I was nowhere, I was nothing, my mouth open round, like a zero, like 0, out of which the baby is born, the words spill, the planet pops, the trees grow, everything rising; real.

In *Lying* I have written a book in which in some cases
I cannot and in other cases I will not say the facts. I
am, after all, the grandchild of Kant, of Heisenberg,
someone who came of age just as the postmodernists
were in their full flower. Postmodernism may have
many problems, but it also has at least one point, a
point that has been driven into my heart and the hearts
of many of my contemporaries, and the point is this:
What matters in knowing and telling yourself is not
the historical truth, which fades as our neurons decay
and stutter, but the narrative truth, which is delight-
fully bendable and politically powerful.

Lying is a book of narrative truth, a book in which
I am more interested in using invention to get to the
heart of things than I am in documenting actual life
occurrences. This means that the text I've created
uses, in some instances, metaphors, most significantly
the metaphor of epilepsy, to express subtleties and
horrors and gaps in my past for which I have never
been able to find the words. Metaphor is the greatest
gift of language, for through it we can propel what
are otherwise wordless experiences into shapes and
sounds. And even if the sounds are not altogether ac-

curate, they do resonate in a heartfelt place we cannot dismiss. That is why it is in this book, although it is not always factually correct, that I feel I have finally, finally been able to tell a tale eluding me for years, a tale I have tried over and over again to utter, the story of my past, of my mother and me, the story of the strange and fitful illnesses claiming most of my moments, the humiliating birth of sexuality, my love of myths and proclivities toward deceit. I have told it all and it is a relief. A relief to put it to rest.

And still. You want to know. What are the real facts about the condition I call epilepsy in the story.

All I can give you is this. I take anticonvulsant medication daily. I have had auras all my life. I have had several symptoms that doctors have diagnosed as consistent with temporal lobe epilepsy. However, diagnosis itself is a narrative phenomenon, because the same symptoms that doctors saw as epilepsy in one era of my life, they saw as borderline personality disorder in another era of my life, and then as posttraumatic stress disorder in yet another era, and as bipolar, and as Munchausen's, and as OCD, and as depression and, once, even, as autism. Autism!

All I know for sure is this. I have been ill much of my life. Illness has claimed my imagination, my brain, my body, and everything I do I see through its feverish scrim. All I can tell you is this. Illness, medicine itself, is the ultimate narrative; there is no truth there, as diagnoses come in and out of vogue as fast as yearly fashions. Line up all the DSMs, the book from which mental health professionals draw their diagnoses, and you will see how they have changed, how they have radically altered from decade to decade, depending upon the Zeitgeist. In this time, right now, in psychiatry, there is a quiet revolution taking place concerning depression. The current story is that depression is a disease springing from a biochemical imbalance. The new story forming is that the evidence for a biochemical imbalance is very poor indeed, and depression may in fact have negligible chemical origins. And so the pendulum swings back.

Therefore, despite the huge proliferation of authoritative illness memoirs in recent years, memoirs that talk about people's personal experiences with Tourette's and postpartum depression and manic depression, memoirs that are often rooted in the latest scientific "evidence," something is amiss. For me, the authority is illusory, the etiologies constructed. When all is said and done, there is only one kind of illness memoir I can see to write, and that's a slippery, playful, impish, exasperating text, shaped, if it could be, like a question mark.

LAUREN SLATER has a master's degree in psychology from Harvard University and a doctorate from Boston University. Her work was chosen for *The Best American Essays/Most Notable Essays* of 1994, 1996, 1997, 1998, and 1999. She is the winner of the 1993 New Letters Literary Award in creative nonfiction and of the 1994 Missouri Review Award. She lives with her husband and daughter in Massachusetts.

This book is set in Fournier, a typeface named for Pierre Simon Fournier, the youngest son of a French printing family. Starting with engraving woodblocks and large capitals, he made several important contributions in the field of type design; he cut and founded all the types himself, pioneered the concepts of the type family, and is said to have cut sixty thousand punches for 147 alphabets of his own design. The Fournier typeface was released in 1925.